TEACHER'S GUIDE

daybook, *n.* a book in which the events of the day are recorded; *specif.* a journal or diary

DAYBOOK
. . . .
of Critical Reading and Writing

GRADE 10

FRAN CLAGGETT

LOUANN REID

RUTH VINZ

Great Source Education Group
a Houghton Mifflin Company
Wilmington, Massachusetts

www.greatsource.com

A u t h o r s

Fran Claggett, currently an educational consultant for schools throughout the country and teacher at Sonoma State University, taught high school English for more than thirty years. She is author of several books, including *Drawing Your Own Conclusions: Graphic Strategies for Reading, Writing, and Thinking* (1992) and *A Measure of Success* (1996).

Louann Reid taught junior and senior high school English, speech, and drama for nineteen years and currently teaches courses for future English teachers at Colorado State University. Author of numerous articles and chapters, her first books were *Learning the Landscape* and *Recasting the Text* with Fran Claggett and Ruth Vinz (1996).

Ruth Vinz, currently a professor and director of English education at Teachers College, Columbia University, taught in secondary schools for twenty-three years. She is author of several books and numerous articles that discuss teaching and learning in the English classroom as well as a frequent presenter, consultant, and co-teacher in schools throughout the country.

Printed in the United States of America

International Standard Book Number: 0-669-46437-6

4 5 6 7 8 9 10 -POO- 04 03 02 01

Great Source wishes to acknowledge the many insights and improvements made to the *Daybooks* thanks to the work of the following teachers and educators.

R e a d e r s

Jay Amberg
Glenbrook South High School
Glenview, Illinois

Joanne Arellanes
Rancho Cordova, California

Nancy Bass
Moore Middle School
Arvada, Colorado

Jim Benny
Sierra Mountain Middle School
Truckee, California

Noreen Benton
Guilderland High School
Altamont, New York

Janet Bertucci
Hawthorne Junior High School
Vernon Hills, Illinois

Jim Burke
Burlingame High School
Burlingame, California

Mary Castellano
Hawthorne Junior High School
Vernon Hills, Illinois

Diego Davalos
Chula Vista High School
Chula Vista, California

Jane Detgen
Daniel Wright Middle School
Lake Forest, Illinois

Michelle Ditzian
Sheperd Junior High School
Deerfield, Illinois

Jenni Dunlap
Highland Middle School
Libertyville, Illinois

Judy Elman
Highland Park High School
Highland Park, Illinois

Mary Ann Evans-Patrick
Fox Valley Writing Project
Oshkosh, Wisconsin

Howard Frishman
Twin Grove Junior High School
Buffalo Grove, Illinois

Kathleen Gaynor
Wheaton, Illinois

Beatrice Gerrish
Bell Middle School
Golden, Colorado

Kathy Glass
San Carlos, California

Alton Greenfield
Minnesota Dept. of Child, Family &
Learning
St. Paul, Minnesota

Sue Hebson
Deerfield High School
Deerfield, Illinois

Carol Jago
Santa Monica High School
Santa Monica, California

Diane Kepner
Oakland, California

Lynne Ludwig
Gregory Middle School
Naperville, Illinois

Joan Markos-Horejs
Fox Valley Writing Project
Oshkosh, Wisconsin

James McDermott
South High Community School
Worcester, Massachusetts

Tim McGee
Worland High School
Worland, Wyoming

Mary Jane Mulholland
Lynn Classical High School
Lynn, Massachusetts

Lisa Myers
Englewood, Colorado

Karen Neilsen
Desert Foothills Middle School
Phoenix, Arizona

Jayne Allen Nichols
El Camino High School
Sacramento, California

Mary Nicolini
Penn Harris High School
Mishawaka, Indiana

Lucretia Pannozzo
John Jay Middle School
Katonah, New York

Robert Pavlick
Marquette University
Milwaukee, Wisconsin

Linda Popp
Gregory Middle School
Naperville, Illinois

Caroline Ratliffe
Fort Bend Instructional School District
Sugar Land, Texas

Guerrino Rich
Akron North High School
Akron, Ohio

Shirley Rosson
Alief Instructional School District
Houston, Texas

Alan Ruter
Glenbrook South High School
Glenview, Illinois

Rene Schillenger
Washington, D.C.

Georgianne Schulte
Oak Park Middle School
Oak Park, Illinois

Carol Schultz
Tinley Park, Illinois

Wendell Schwartz
Adlai E. Stevenson High School
Lincolnshire, Illinois

Lynn Snell
Oak Grove School
Green Oaks, Illinois

Hildi Spritzer
Oakland, California

Bill Stone
Plano Senior High School
Plano, Texas

Barbara Thompson
Hazelwood School
Florissant, Missouri

Elma Torres
Orange Grove Instructional School
District Orange Grove, Texas

Bill Weber
Libertyville High School
Libertyville, Illinois

Darby Williams
Sacramento, California

Hillary Zunin
Napa High School
Napa, California

Table of Contents

O v e r v i e w

What is a daybook and what is it good for? These are the first questions asked about this series, *Daybooks of Critical Reading and Writing.*

The answer is that a daybook is a keepable, journal-like book that helps improve students' reading and writing. *Daybooks* are a tool to promote daily reading and writing in classrooms. By immersing students in good literature and by asking them to respond creatively to it, the *Daybooks* combine critical reading and creative, personal response to literature.

The literature in each *Daybook* has been chosen to complement the selections commonly found in anthologies and the most commonly taught novels. Most of the literature selections are brief and designed to draw students into them by their brevity and high-interest appeal. In addition, each passage has a literary quality that will be probed in the lesson.

Each lesson focuses on a specific aspect of critical reading—that is, the reading skills used by good readers. These aspects of critical reading are summarized in closing statements positioned at the end of each lesson. To organize this wide-ranging analysis into critical reading, the authors have constructed a framework called the "Angles of Literacy."

This framework organizes the lessons and units in the *Daybook.* The five Angles of Literacy described here are:

- marking or annotating the text
- examining the story connections
- looking at a text from multiple perspectives
- studying the language and craft of a text
- focusing on individual authors

The Angles of Literacy are introduced in the first cluster of the *Daybook* and then explored in greater depth in subsequent clusters.

The *Daybook* concept was developed to help teachers with a number of practical concerns:

1. To introduce daily (or at least weekly) critical reading and writing into classrooms

2. To fit into the new configurations offered by block scheduling

3. To create a literature book students can own, allowing them to mark up the literature and write as they read

4. To make an affordable literature book that students can carry home

How to Use the Daybook

As the *Daybooks* were being developed, more than fifty teachers commented on and reviewed the lesson concept and individual lessons and units. From their comments several main uses for the *Daybooks* emerged.

1. Block Scheduling

Daybook activities were designed to accommodate block-scheduled class periods. With longer periods, teachers commented on the need to introduce two to four parts to each "block," one of which would be a *Daybook* lesson. The brief, self-contained lessons fit perfectly at the beginning or end of a block and could be used to complement or build upon another segment of the day.

2. Electives

With the advent of block scheduling, more electives are being added to the curriculum. Course slots now exist once again for poetry, reading for college, creative writing, and contemporary writers. Teachers found a number of different course slots in which to use the *Daybooks*, mostly because of the strong combination of literature, critical reading, and creative writing.

3. Core Reading List

For high schools guided by a list of core readings, the *Daybooks* offered a convenient way to add some daily writing and critical reading instruction to classes. Plus, the emphasis on newer, contemporary writers seemed to these teachers to open up the traditional curriculum with new voices.

4. Supplementing an Anthology

For literature teachers using older anthologies, the *Daybook* offers an easy, economical means of updating their literature curriculums. The multitude of newer, contemporary authors and wide range of multicultural authors added nicely to literature classes.

The reviewers of the *Daybooks* proved that no two classrooms are alike. While each was unique in its own way, every teacher found uses for the *Daybook* lessons in the classroom. In the end, the usefulness of the *Daybooks* derived from the blend of elements they offer:

- direct instruction on how to read critically
- regular and explicit practice in marking up and annotating texts
- "writing to learn" activities for each day or week
- great selections from contemporary (and often multicultural) literature
- in-depth instruction in how to read literature and write effectively about it

Organization of the Daybooks

Each *Daybook* has 16 units, or clusters, of five lessons. The 80 lessons afford daily work over a single semester or work two or three times each week for an entire year. A lesson is designed to last approximately 30 minutes, although some lessons will surely extend longer depending on how energetically students attack the writing activities. But the intent throughout was to create brief, potent lessons that integrate quality literature, critical reading instruction, and writing.

The unifying concept behind these lessons is the angles of literacy—the idea that a selection can be approached from at least five directions:

- by annotating and marking up the text
- by analyzing the story connections in the literature
- by examining the text from different perspectives
- by studying the language and craft of the writer
- by focusing closely on all of the aspects of a single writer's work

Each angle is introduced in the first half of the book, and then explored again in somewhat more sophisticated fashion in the second half of the book. The opening unit of the *Daybook* introduces all of the angles and demonstrates their application.

A lesson typically begins with an introduction and leads quickly into a literary selection. Occasionally the purpose is to direct students' attention to a specific aspect of the selection; but just as often students are asked to read and formulate a response on their own. By looking closely at the selection, students are able to discover what can be learned through careful reading. Students are led to look again at the selection and to respond analytically, reflectively, and creatively to what they have read.

boldface terms in glossary

personification, a FIGURE OF SPEECH in which an author embodies an inanimate object with human characteristics. "The rock stubbornly refused to move" is an example.

~~rs~~pective, see POINT OF VIEW.

focus on critical reading

lesson title

longer, interpretive response to literature

unit title

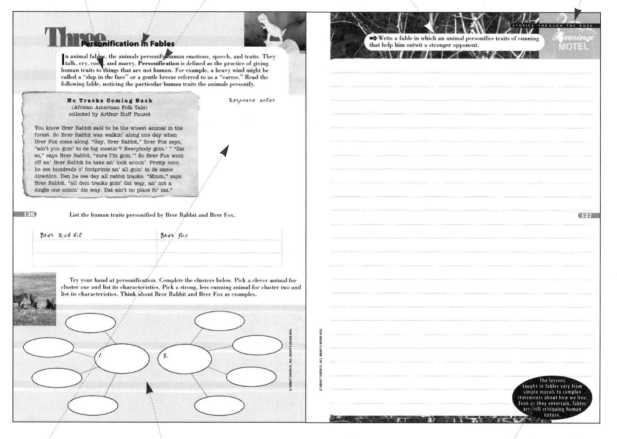

space for annotations

initial response activity

summary statement

Frequently Asked Questions

One benefit of the extensive field-testing of the *Daybooks* was to highlight right at the beginning several questions about the *Daybooks*.

1. What is a daybook anyway?

A daybook used to be "a book in which daily transactions are recorded" or "a diary." Most recently, the word has been used to mean "journal." To emphasize the daily reading and writing, the authors chose the word *daybook* rather than *journal*. And, indeed, the *Daybooks* are much more than journals, in that they include literature selections and instruction in critical reading.

2. Are students supposed to write in the *Daybook*?

Yes, definitely. Only by physically marking the text will students become active readers. To interact with a text and take notes as an active reader, students must write in their *Daybooks*. Students will have a written record of their thoughts, questions, brainstorms, annotations, and creative responses. The immediacy of reading and responding on the page is an integral feature of the *Daybooks*. Students will also benefit from the notebook-like aspect, allowing them to double back to earlier work, see progress, store ideas, and record responses. The *Daybook* serves, in a way, like a portfolio. It is one simple form of portfolio assessment.

3. Can I photocopy these lessons?

No, unfortunately, you cannot. The selections, instruction, and activities are protected by copyright. To copy them infringes on the rights of the authors of the selections and the book. Writers such as Octavio Paz, Toni Morrison, and Ray Bradbury have granted permission for the use of their work in the *Daybook* and to photocopy their work violates their copyright.

4. Can I skip around in the *Daybook*?

Yes, absolutely. The *Daybooks* were designed to allow teachers maximum flexibility. You can start with some of the later clusters (or units) and then pick up the earlier ones later on in the year. Or you can teach a lesson from here and one from there. But the optimum order of the book is laid out in the table of contents, and students will most likely see the logic and continuity of the book when they start at the beginning and proceed in order.

5. What is "annotating a text"? Are students supposed to write in the margin of the book?

Annotating refers to underlining parts of a text, circling words or phrases, highlighting with a colored marker, or taking notes in the margin. Students begin their school years marking up books in kindergarten and end, often in college, writing in the margins of their texts or highlighting key passages. Yet in the years in between—the majority of their school years—students are often forbidden from writing in their books, even though it represents a natural kinesthetic aid for memory and learning.

6. Why were these literature selections chosen?

The *Daybooks* are intended to complement high school classrooms, most of which use literature anthologies or have core lists of novels that they teach. In either instance, the literature taught tends to be traditional. Adding contemporary selections is the best way to complement existing curriculums.

The literature was also chosen to illustrate the lesson idea. (A lesson on story characters, for example, needed to present two or three strong characters for study.) So, in addition to being chosen for appeal for students, selections illustrate the specific aspect of critical reading focused on in that lesson.

7. What are the art and photos supposed to represent?

The art program for the *Daybooks* features the work of outstanding contemporary photographers. These photos open each unit and set the tone. Then, within each lesson, a number of smaller, somewhat enigmatic images are used. The purpose behind these images is not to illustrate what is happening in the literature or even to represent an interpretation of it. Rather, the hope is to stretch students' minds, hinting at connections, provoking the imagination, jarring loose a random thought or two about the selection. And, of course, the hope is that students will respond favorably to contemporary expressions of creativity.

8. What are the boldface terms in the lesson all about?

The terms boldfaced in the lessons appear in a glossary in the back of the *Daybook*. The glossary includes key literary terms
  1) that are used in the *Daybook* lessons and
  2) that students are likely to encounter in literature classes.

The glossary is another resource for students to use in reading and reacting to the literature.

Correlation to Writers INC

Like the *Writers INC* handbook, the *Daybooks* will appeal to certain teachers who need versatile, flexible materials and who place a premium on books with high student appeal. Some teachers, by nature, are more eclectic in their teaching approach: others more consistent and patterned. Some teachers place a premium on student interest and relevance more than on structured, predictable lessons. The *Daybooks*, like *Writers INC*, are directed at more eclectic teachers and classrooms.

The *Daybooks* are organized to allow maximum flexibility. You can pick an individual lesson or cluster of lessons in order to feature a certain author or literary selection. Or, you may want to concentrate on a particular area of critical reading. In either case, the *Daybooks*, like *Writers INC,* allow you to pick up the book and use it for days or weeks at a time, then leave it, perhaps to teach a novel or longer writing project, and then return to it again later in the semester. You, not the text, set the classroom agenda.

Another great similarity between the *Daybooks* and the *Writers INC* handbook lies in the approach to writing. Both begin from the premise that writing is, first and foremost, a means of discovery. "Writing to learn" is the common expression for this idea. Only by expression can we discover what lies within us. *Writers INC* introduces this idea in its opening chapter, and the *Daybooks*, by promoting daily writing, give you the tool to make writing a consistent, regular feature of your classes.

But the *Daybooks* only start students on a daily course of reading and writing. Individual writing assignments are initiated but not carried through to final drafts. The purpose of writing in the *Daybooks* is mostly one of discovery, creative expression, clarification of ideas or interpretations, and idea generation. The *Daybooks* are intended to be starting points, places to ruminate and organize thoughts about literature, as opposed to offering definitive instructions about how to craft an essay or write a persuasive letter. That's where *Writers INC* comes in. It picks up where the *Daybooks* leave off, providing everything students need to create a polished essay or literary work.

The accompanying chart correlates writing assignments in the *Daybooks* to *Writers INC.*

Daybook Lesson	Writing Activity	Writers INC reference
Angles of Literacy		
1. Interactions with the Text	summarize a poem	444, 494, 497
2. Story Connections	write a news story	294–297, 299
3. Shifting Perspectives	describe an event	294–297, 299
4. Language and Craft	write a double-entry log	279–282, 419–420
5. Focus on the Writer	interpret a poem	410–411, 414, 444

Daybook Lesson	Writing Activity	Writers INC reference
The Lessons Stories Teach		
1. Patterns in Stories	write a short story	312, 319, 323
2. Symbolic Meaning	respond to a poem	398–400, 444, 494
3. Understanding New Symbols	write a short essay	117, 410–412, 416
4. Familiar Symbols in Unfamiliar Places	draw pictures	311–312
5. A Network of Symbols in Story	write a story ending	312–313, 319
Heroes and Heroines		
1. Who Is a Hero?	write a speech	311–312, 336
2. Who Is a Heroine?	compose a dialogue	331–332, 335
3. Models for Living	write an essay about a person	117, 304–305
4. Are Heroes Always Admirable?	write a poem	311–312, 313
5. Who Are My Heroes and Heroines?	write a tribute	117, 313
New Ways of Seeing and Knowing		
1. Seeing the Details	respond to nonfiction	282, 398–400, 494
2. Seeing the Literal Meaning	sketch a place	311–312
3. Observing and Interpreting	make a chart	398–400, 494
4. Looking Beneath the Surface	write a paragraph	102–104, 106, 110–111
5. Comprehending Critically	write about a memoir	337–340, 398–400
Perspectives on a Subject: The Vietnam War		
1. Presenting a Subject	evaluate nonfiction	135, 398–400, 545
2. Using Supporting Material	examine historical writing	398–400, 560
3. Firsthand Experience	compare and contrast two pieces	398–400, 548–5549
4. Different Genres	write a paragraph	414, 444
5. Comparing Perspectives	rewite a piece	297, 313, 423

Daybook Lesson	Writing Activity	Writers INC reference
Shades of Meaning		
1. Close Reading	write a short essay	117, 337–339, 340–353
2. Comparing to Define	write a poem	311–313, 363
3. Scientific and Poetic Language	examine nonfiction	398–400, 552–553
4. Establishing Mood	draw a picture	311–312, 496
5. Visualizing Words	write about a poem	398–400, 444
Words in Context		
1. Sensory Language	write a paragraph	102–104, 106, 138
2. Familiar Words in Unfamiliar Ways	create a scene	111, 138, 311–312
3. Words and Social History	write a description	136, 279–282, 337–340
4. Simple Words, Complex Ideas	write about an essay	398–400, 411–412
5. The Power of the Present Tense	write about an object	66–68, 138, 338–340
John Steinbeck		
1. The Unfinished Children of Nature	create a chart	398–402, 494
2. Character Relationships	write about characters	398–402, 415–416
3. The Unfinished Child as an Adult	analyze a passage	410–412, 415
4. Characters as Witnesses	explore characters	398–400, 411–412
5. The Perfectibility of Man	examine an author's idea	120, 415
Essentials of Reading		
1. Thinking With the Writer	write an ending for a story	312, 319, 330
2. Considering the Theme	interpret a short story	356, 412, 415
3. Reading Between the Lines	write an introductory paragraph	311–312, 319, 415
4. Doubling Back	explore style and language	60, 412, 415
5. Author's Purpose	write a letter to the editor	339, 393, 400–401

Daybook Lesson	Writing Activity	Writers INC reference
Stories Through the Ages		
1. Lessons in Animal Fables	write a paragraph	102–104, 412
2. Fables in Cultural Context	write a contemporary fable	311–312, 319, 330
3. Personification in Fables	write a fable	311–312, 319, 323–327
4. Characteristics of Tricksters	extend a fable	311–312, 319, 330
5. Stories of Animals Today	respond to an essay	339–340, 398–402
Transforming Stories		
1. The Changing Story	write sentences about a story	89–101, 398–402
2. Recasting a Story	compose song lyrics	311–312, 495–496, 554
3. Reinterpretations	write a paragraph	102–104, 412, 550
4. Timeless Stories	respond to a story	102–104, 398–402
5. Changing Perspectives	write a fairy tale	311–312, 319, 554
Asking Questions about Poems		
1. Literal Understanding	develop questions about a poem	444, 557
2. Layers of Meaning	explain a poem's meaning	410–412, 414, 444
3. Asking Interpretive Questions	write a paragraph	104, 410–412, 444
4. Language and Structure	write about a poem	410–412, 444
5. Speculative Questions	write a poem	311–312, 554
Text and Subtext		
1. Supplying the Background	write a diary entry	311–312, 320
2. Shifting Point of View	rewrite a story	311–312, 423, 554
3. Understanding Irony	complete a chart	398–400, 421
4. Examining Assumptions	write a paragraph	102–104, 400–402
5. Understanding Tone	write a poem	311–312, 313

Daybook Lesson	Writing Activity	Writers INC reference
Poetry and Craft		
1. Light Verse	write a limerick	311–312, 313
2. Reading a Poem for Meaning	examine a poem's meaning	400, 402, 444
3. The Italian Sonnet	interpret a poem's form	398, 400, 444
4. The Shakespearean Sonnet	analyze a poem	398, 400, 444
5. The Modern Sonnet	reflect on poetry	337–340, 343
Writing from Models: Tone		
1. Reading for Tone	extend a poem	312–313, 330
2. Understanding Tone	write a letter	373–376, 400
3. Comparing Poems	compare poems	402, 444, 550
4. Using Metaphors	respond to a poem	400, 402, 444
5. The Paralog	write a paralog	330, 400, 402, 444
Zora Neale Hurston		
1. The Autobiographical Narrator	write a paragraph	102–104, 402, 444
2. In Search of Her People's History	write a story	312, 319, 330
3. Creating Characters	examine an author's ideas	102–104, 400, 560–562
4. Multiple Points of View	rewrite fiction	319, 330, 332
5. The Writer's Themes	write a short essay	118–123, 128, 400

Angles of Literacy

by Louann Reid

When we view something of potential value, such as a diamond or an antique vase, we often examine it from all sides. We hold it up and slowly turn it, looking first at the front, then the sides and back. Combining information from each perspective, we construct a fuller picture of the object and its worth.

Similarly, we can examine a concept or idea from several angles, or perspectives, using a variety of approaches to understand a complex concept. Perhaps no concept in education is more complex—or more important—than literacy.

"Literacy" is frequently defined as the ability to read and write. But people also need to be able to read critically, write effectively, draw diagrams, collaborate with others, listen carefully, and understand complex instructions. In short, literacy means being able to do whatever is required to communicate effectively in a variety of situations. Angles of Literacy is the term we use in these *Daybooks* to identify five approaches to becoming literate.

THE FIVE ANGLES

The Angles of Literacy are major perspectives from which to examine a text. Strategies within each angle further define each one. Activities in the *Daybooks* provide students with multiple opportunities to become autonomous users of the strategies on other literature that they will encounter.

The angles are listed on page seven in an order that reflects the way that readers and writers first engage with the text. They are encouraged to move gradually from that initial engagement to a more evaluative or critical stance where they study the author's language and craft, life and work. They critique the texts they read and consider what other critics have written. Moving from engagement through interpretation to evaluation is the process that Louise Rosenblatt and later reader-response critics advocate.

In our own work with secondary school students, we have repeatedly seen the value of encouraging students to read and write using all three stages—engagement, interpretation, evaluation. We also know that students sometimes begin at a different stage in the process—perhaps with interpretation rather than engagement. So, our five angles are not meant to be a hierarchy. Students may begin their engagement with the text using any angle and proceed in any order. Depending on the text and the context, readers might start with making personal connections to the stories in an essay. If the text is by an author that the students know well, they might naturally begin by comparing this work to the author's other works.

STRATEGIES

Strategies are plans or approaches to learning. By using some strategies over and over, students can learn to comprehend any text. The *Daybook* activities, such as annotating or visualizing a specific poem, story, or essay, provide students multiple opportunities to develop these strategies. From using this scaffolding students gradually become more independent readers and, ultimately, fully literate.

Because strategies are employed through activities, it may seem at first that they are the same thing. Yet, it is important to remember that a strategy is a purposeful plan. When, as readers, we select a strategy such as underlining key phrases, we have selected this action deliberately to help us differentiate between important information and unimportant information. We may use a double-entry log (an activity) to identify the metaphors in a poem. Our purpose in doing so is to understand figurative language (a strategy). Strategies are purposeful plans, often consisting of one or more activities, to help us comprehend and create.

At the end of each lesson, the strategies are explicitly stated. In a sentence or two, the main point of the activity is noted. When students complete all 80 lessons in a daybook, they will have 80 statements of what they, as active readers, can do to read critically and write effectively.

Reflection is a vital component in helping students understand the use of strategies. After using a particular strategy, students need to step back and consider how the strategy worked or did not. They might think about how an approach or a strategy can change their understanding of what they read and write. Students might ask themselves a series of questions such as: What have I done? What have I learned? What would I do differently next time? How did the angle or strategy affect my understanding? What would I understand differently if I had changed the angle or the strategy?

ACTIVITIES

Each lesson in these *Daybooks* contains activities for students. From rereading to discussing with a partner to making a story chart, students learn how to become better critical readers and more effective writers. Many activities encourage students to write to learn. Other activities encourage students to increase their understanding of a text by visualizing it in a sketch or a graphic organizer. But, as much as possible, the *Daybooks* try to encourage students to make a creative written response with a poem, some dialogue, a character sketch, or some other creative assignment.

We have selected activities that work particularly well with the texts in the lesson and with the strategies we want students to develop. However, as you will see when you and your students use the *Daybooks*, there are several possible activities that could reinforce a particular strategy. You may want to have students try some of these activities, such as making a story chart or using a double-entry log, when they read other texts in class. This would also be another opportunity to have students ask themselves the reflective questions.

A n g l e s   o f   L i t e r a c y

Angle of Vision	Strategies	Selected Activities
Interacting with a Text	• underlining key phrases • writing questions or comments in the margin • noting word patterns and repetitions • circling unknown words • keeping track of the story or idea as it unfolds	• Write down initial impressions. • Re-read. • Write a summary of the poem. • Generate two questions and one "certainty." Then, discuss the questions and statement in a small group.
Making Connections to the Stories within a Text	• paying attention to the stories being told • connecting the stories to one's own experience • speculating on the meaning or significance of incidents	• Make a story chart with three columns—incident in the poem, significance of the incident, related incident in my life. • Write a news story of events behind the story in the poem.

Shifting Perspectives to Examine a Text from Many Points of View	• examining the point of view
	• changing the point of view
	• exploring various versions of an event
	• forming interpretations
	• comparing texts
	• asking "what if" questions
		• Discuss with a partner or small group how you might read a poem differently if:
		  the speaker were female
		  you believe the speaker is a parent
		• Rewrite the text from a different point of view.

Studying the Language and Craft of a Text	• understanding figurative language • looking at the way the author uses words • modeling the style of other writers • studying various kinds of literature	• Use a double-entry log to identify metaphors and the qualities implied by the comparison. • Examine the title of the poem and its relationship to the text.
Focusing on the Writer's Life and Work	• reading what the author says about the writing • reading what others say • making inferences about the connections between an author's life and work • analyzing the writer's style • paying attention to repeated themes and topics in the work by one author	• Read about the poet's life. Then make an inference chart to record evidence from the poet's life, an inference, a comparison to the poem. • Write an evaluation of the poem. Then read what one or more critics have said about the poem or poet. Finally, write a short response, either agreeing or disagreeing with the critic. Support your ideas with textual evidence.

Responding to Literature Through Writing

by Ruth Vinz

We have found that students' encounters with literature are enriched when they write their way toward understanding. The writing activities in the *Daybooks* are intended to help students explore and organize their ideas and reactions during and after reading. We try to make use of the exploratory and clarifying roles of writing through various activities.

Exploratory assignments include those through which students question, analyze, annotate, connect, compare, personalize, emulate, map, or chart aspects in the literary selections. Generally these assignments aid students' developing interpretations and reactions to the subjects, themes, or literary devices in the literature they are reading. Other writing activities offer students the opportunity to clarify their understanding of what they've read. These assignments lead students to look at other perspectives, determine the significance of what they read, and prioritize, interpret, question, and reflect on initial impressions. Further, students are asked to create literature of their own as a way of applying the concepts they're learning. Writing to clarify also involves students in reflection, where they are asked to think about their reactions and working hypotheses. Taken together, the writing activities represent a series of strategies that students can apply to the complex task of reading literature.

The writing activities included in the *Daybooks* start students on the path toward understanding. We did not take it as the function of the writing activities in this book to lead students through the writing process toward final, finished drafts. Although examples of extensions are included here in the Teacher's Guide, the writing in the *Daybooks* introduces first draft assignments that may lead into more formal writing if you, as the teacher, so choose.

You will have your own ideas about assisting students with the writing activities or extending the writing beyond the *Daybooks*. We think it's important for you to remind students that the writing in which they engage is useful for their reading outside the *Daybooks*. For example, students may use various types of maps, charts, or diagrams introduced in the *Daybooks* when they read a novel. They may find that the response notes become a strategy they use regularly. Once exposed to imitation and modeling, students may find these useful tools for understanding an author's style, language, or structure. If your students develop a conscious awareness of the strategies behind the particular writing activities, they can apply these in other reading situations.

Writing assignments to explore and to clarify students' developing interpretations are incorporated in two types of activities, both of which are elaborated on below.

WRITING ABOUT LITERATURE

You will find activities in every cluster of lessons that call upon students to write about the literature they are reading. We developed these writing assignments to help facilitate, stimulate, support, and shape students' encounters with literature. We think the assignments have four purposes:

(1) to connect the literature to the students' personal experiences; (2) to re-examine the text for various purposes (language and craft, connections with other texts, shifting perspectives, developing interpretations); (3) to develop hypotheses, judgments, and critical interpretations; (4) to apply the idea behind the lesson to a new literary text or situation.

The types of writing we have used to fulfill these purposes are:

1. Response Notes

Students keep track of their initial responses to the literature by questioning, annotating, and marking up the text in various ways. The response notes are used to get students in the habit of recording what they are thinking while reading. Seldom do we begin by telling them what and how to write in this space. Many times we circle back and ask them to build on what they have written with a particular focus or way of responding. In the response notes, students are encouraged to make personal connections, re-examine text, jot down ideas for their own writing, and monitor their changing responses.

2. Personal Narrative

Students write personal stories that connect or relate to what they have read. In some cases, the narratives tell the stories of students' prior reading experiences or how a literary selection relates to their life experiences. Other activities use personal narrative to apply and refine students' understanding of narrative principles.

3. Idea Fund

Students collect ideas for writing—catalogs, lists, charts, clusters, diagrams, double-entry logs, sketches, or maps. These forms of idea gathering are useful for analyzing particular literary selections and will aid the initial preparation for longer pieces of critical analysis.

4. Short Response

Students write summaries; paraphrase main themes or ideas; and compose paragraphs of description, exposition, explanation, evaluation, and interpretation.

5. Analysis

Students write short analyses that take them beyond summarizing the literary selection or their personal reactions to it. The analytic activities engage students in recognizing symbols and figures of speech and the links between events, characters, or images. Again, these short analytical responses are intended to prepare students for longer, critical interpretation that you, as a teacher, might assign.

6. Speculation

Students' speculations are encouraged by writing activities that engage them in predicting, inferring, and imagining. "What if…," "How might…," and "Imagine that. . ." are all ways in which students are invited to see further possibilities in the literature they read.

Students use writing to record and reflect on their reactions and interpretations. At times, students are asked to share their writing with others. Such sharing is another form of reflection through which students have an opportunity to "see again" their own work in the context of what others have produced.

The writing activities in the *Daybooks* will help students connect what they read with what they experience and with what they write, and also to make connections between the literary selections and literary techniques. The activities encourage students to experiment with a range of forms, choose a range of focuses, and reflect on what they have learned from these. We hope the writing serves to give students access to a kind of literary experience they can value and apply in their future reading

WRITING LITERATURE

Within a literary work, readers find a writer's vision, but readers also co-create the vision along with the writer and learn from his or her craft. We've asked our students to write literature of their own as a way of responding to what they read. Through writing literature, students can explore facets of the original work or use the techniques of a variety of authors. Here are a number of the activities introduced in the *Daybooks*:

1. Take the role of writer

Students write imaginative reconstructions of gaps in a text by adding another episode, adding dialogue, rewriting the ending, adding a section before or after the original text, adding characters, changing the setting, or creating dream sequences. Such imaginative entries into the text require that students apply their knowledge of the original.

2. Imitation and Modeling

The idea of modeling and imitation is not new. Writers learn from other writers. The modeling activities are intended to help students "read like a writer." In these activities, students experiment with nuances of expression, syntactic and other structural principles, and apply their knowledge of literary devices (for example, *rhythm, imagery, metaphor*). One goal in educating students with literature is to make explicit what writers do. One way to achieve the goal is to provide models that illustrate various principles of construction.

3. Original Pieces

Students write poems, character sketches, monologues, dialogues, episodes, vignettes, and descriptions as a way to apply the knowledge about language and craft they are gaining through their reading.

4. Living Others' Perspectives

Writing from others' points of view encourages students to step beyond self to imagine other perspectives. Students write from a character's point of view, compose diary entries or letters, explain others' positions or opinions, and other reactions to a situation. These writing activities encourage students to explore the concerns of others and to project other perspectives through their writing.

The writing becomes a record of students' developing and changing ideas about literature. By the time students have finished all of the writing in this book, they will have used writing strategies that can assist them in all future reading.

Reading, Writing, and Assessment

by Fran Claggett

As teachers, we all cope with the complexities of assessing student performance. We must be careful readers of student work, attentive observers of student participation in various activities, and focused writers in responding to student work. We must understand the value of rewarding what students do well and encouraging them to improve. Above all, we need to make the criteria for assessment clear to students.

THE DAYBOOKS

The *Daybooks* provide visible accounts of many aspects of the reading process. Students record all the various permutations of active reading and writing. In the current view of most teachers and researchers, reading is a process of constructing meaning through transactions with a text. In this view, the individual reader assumes responsibility for interpreting a text guided not only by the language of the text but also by the associations, cultural experiences, and prior knowledge that the reader brings to the interpretive task. Meaning does not reside solely within the words on the page. Our view of reading emphasizes the role of the reader. Construction of meaning, rather than the gaining and displaying of knowledge should be the goal of reading instruction. This rule is reflected throughout the *Daybooks*, which guide students in how to read, respond to, interpret, and reflect on carefully selected works of literature.

Within these lessons, students interact with a text from five angles of literacy. The *Daybooks* make it possible for both students and teachers to track students' increasing sophistication in using the angles to make sense of their reading. Through the strategies presented in the lessons, students learn to express their understanding of a text. They will do such things as show their understanding of figurative language and the importance of form; write about how characters are developed and change; and demonstrate their understanding of how a piece of literature develops.

THE ROLE OF THE TEACHER

The teacher is critical to the *Daybook* agenda. Conceivably, a teacher could pass out the *Daybooks* and turn the students loose, but that would not result in the carefully guided reading and writing that is intended. Rather, the teachers are central to student success. Because of the format of the *Daybooks*, lessons are short, each taking no more than a normal class period. They are intended to be complete in themselves, yet most teachers will see that there are numerous opportunities for extensions, elaborations, further readings, group work, and writing. The Teacher's Guide provides some suggestions; you will think of many others. The *Daybooks* offer guidelines for reading and thinking, for writing and drawing used in the service of reading. They also provide many opportunities for students to write pieces of their own, modeling, responding, interpreting, and reflecting on the pieces that they have read. Many of these pieces might lead to later revision, refining, group response, and editing. It is the teacher, however, who knows the students well enough to see which pieces would be worthwhile to work with and which it is best to leave as exercises rather than completed works.

In assessing the *Daybooks*, it is important to remember to look at the students' growing facility with the processes of reading. As is true with all learning, there will be false starts, abandoned practices, and frustrations, yet also illuminations, progress, and occasional epiphanies. No music teacher ever graded every attempt at mastering a piece of music. We, too, must resist the urge—honed by years of assessing only products or finished papers—of overassessing the *Daybooks*. We must consider them the place where students are free to think things through, change their minds, even start over. But you can be alert to what the student is doing well, what is frustrating, what needs more time. To that end, we have provided a chart which may be useful in getting a sense of how students are progressing in using angles of literacy. By duplicating the chart for each student, you can track progress through the lessons. We would like to encourage the idea of jotting down notations as you work with students during the class period or look over the *Daybooks* after class. In this way, you can amass a sizable amount of information over a grading period. Coupled with a student self-assessment such as the one included here, you will have tangible evidence of achievement in the *Daybooks*.

STUDENT SELF-ASSESSMENT

A student self-assessment chart is a useful adjunct to the teacher chart. This particular format works well as it asks students to consider interest, value, and participation as well as quality.

Followed by the self-assessment essay, it provides valuable insight into the student's sense of accomplishment.

INDIVIDUAL STUDENT EIGHT-WEEK ASSESSMENT CHART

The columns for each week's lessons can be used in different ways. We suggest the number system: a 5 for insightful, imaginative thinking or responding, a 1 for a minimal attempt. Some teachers prefer the check, check-plus, check-minus system. There is even room, if you turn the chart sideways, to make some notations.

A n g l e s   o f   L i t e r a c y

INTERACTING WITH A TEXT	I	II	III	IV	V	VI	VII	VIII
The student demonstrates understanding by using interactive strategies such as:								
underlining key phrases								
writing questions or comments in the margin								
noting word patterns and repetitions								
circling unknown words								
keeping track of ideas as they unfold								

MAKING CONNECTIONS	I	II	III	IV	V	VI	VII	VIII
The student makes connections to the stories with a text by:								
paying attention to the stories in the text								
connecting ideas and themes in the text to personal ideas, experience, feelings, and knowledge								
making connections to other texts, movies, television shows, or other media								

SHIFTING PERSPECTIVES	I	II	III	IV	V	VI	VII	VIII
The student is able to shift perspectives to examine a text from many points of view. When prompted, the student will engage in such strategies as:								
examining the point of view								
changing the point of view								
exploring various versions of an event and forming interpretations								
comparing texts and responding to "what if" questions to deepen understanding								

STUDYING THE LANGUAGE AND CRAFT OF A TEXT	I	II	III	IV	V	VI	VII	VIII

The student will demonstrate an understanding of the way language and craft operate in a text. Specifically, the student will show how:

imagery, metaphor, and figurative language are central to literature

demonstrate an understanding of how an author's vocabulary and use of language are integral to the overall work

use modeling to demonstrate an understanding of style and form

demonstrate understanding of various genres and forms of literature

FOCUSING ON THE WRITER	I	II	III	IV	V	VI	VII	VIII

The student will demonstrate a rich understanding of a single writer's work, including:

interpreting short texts by the author

making inferences about the connections between an author's life and work

analyzing the writer's style

drawing conclusions about repeated themes and topics in an author's work

evaluating a text or comparing works by the same author

END OF TERM STUDENT SELF-ASSESSMENT CHART

Fill out the chart by naming or describing the work you have completed in the *Daybooks*. Since the *Daybooks* are focused on the reading of and writing about literature, it might be useful to list the actual texts you have read. To measure your achievement, think about the work you did as you explored the angles of vision for each text.

For each item, use the numbers 1 (low) to 5 (high) to indicate the four aspects of your involvement. Following completion of the chart, write the Self-Assessment Essay.

WORKS OF LITERATURE READ	LEVEL OF INTEREST	LEVEL OF VALUE	DEGREE OF PARTICIPATION	QUALITY OF PARTICIPATION

STUDENT SELF-ASSESSMENT ESSAY

After you have filled out this chart, write a self-evaluation essay, reflecting on your work in the *Daybooks* for the past term and articulating ideas about what you hope to achieve in the next. Refer specifically to the texts listed in the chart, elaborating on your assessment of a text's interest or value, commenting on reasons for the degree of your involvement, or explaining why you have assessed the quality of your work as you have.

Modeling: An Overview

by Fran Claggett

The overriding goal in modeling is to help students become discerning readers and inventive, perceptive writers. Modeling works well with students of all ability levels, whether homogeneously or heterogeneously grouped. It is especially effective in working with second-language students. My own classroom experience, as well as testimony from writers and researchers, indicates that modeling closely resembles the natural stages we go through in the acquisition of language. Many writers have talked about how, during their formative years, they either consciously or unconsciously imitated the styles of other writers whom they admired. Here, I will focus on the metacognitive aspects of modeling, making the processes of thinking and learning explicit for students, urging them to explore their own ways of making sense not only of what they read but what they write.

USING MODELING IN THE CLASSROOM

Through various modeling experiences, students learn the relationships among form, structure, and style. They learn to slow down their reading in order to appreciate the ways authors create specific effects. A critical aspect of using modeling with all students is the selection of the work to be modeled. The teacher must be clear on the focus of the assignment, allow for the margin of success by selecting works for modeling that are within the students' grasp, and make certain that students enter into the metacognitive aspect of the exercise.

Some of the ways that modeling can be integrated into classroom assignments:

1. As a catalyst for writing, particularly for reluctant writers. It immediately provides a structure and takes away much of the threat of the blank page.

2. As an introduction to poetry. Again, much of the onus is gone when students first model a poem, then discover the form by analyzing their own work as well as the original.

3. To encourage close reading of a text. As part of the study of a novel—particularly a difficult one stylistically—have students choose a representative passage (they decide what is representative), model it, then do a structural analysis of it. This exercise enhances both their understanding of the content of the original (it slows down their reading) and their grasp of the author's style. Students often work together in pairs or groups on this activity.

4. To teach awareness of diction. Choose a passage and, as a class, analyze its tone by exploring the use of diction, detail, and syntax. They might even write an analysis of the passage. Either after or before the analysis, students choose a different subject from that of the original and emulate the passage, working consciously to create a particular tone or effect. Students can also write emulations of each other's work, accompanied by an analysis and critique.

5. As a way of teaching English language sentence patterns to second-language learners. By modeling, students are able to internalize the natural flow of English sentences.

6. As part of an intensive author study. Students read a variety of works (short stories, essays, poems, novels, plays) by a single author. They select sections they believe to be representative of the author's style and analyze them from the standpoint of diction, tone, and main idea. They should model a short section. Their final piece in this assignment, which also involves secondary source biographical research, is to write a full imitation of the style of this author, showing through their choice of subject matter, genre, syntax, voice, and tone that they have developed and internalized a familiarity with the author's style.

KINDS OF MODELING TAUGHT IN THE DAYBOOKS

Emulation	replace word for word by function
Spinoff Modeling	respond to original content; retain tone, perhaps first line
Fixed Form Modeling	follow the pattern or form of the original (e.g., a sonnet)
Structural Modeling	model the thought progressions of the original
The Paralog	create a parallel dialogue with the author
Style Modeling	write a substantial piece in the style of an author

Unit Overview

"Angles of Literacy" introduces students to a variety of ways to respond to a text. As students explore the poetry of Seamus Heaney, they will learn how to mark a text, make connections to the stories being told, recognize various points of view, and pay attention to a work's structure and language. In addition, students will discover how having information about a writer's life and work can enrich their understanding of what they read.

Literature Focus

	Lesson	Literature
1.	Interactions with the Text	**Seamus Heaney,** "Digging" (Poetry)
		Seamus Heaney, "Blackberry-Picking" (Poetry)
2.	Story Connections	**Seamus Heaney,** "Mid-Term Break" (Poetry)
3.	Shifting Perspectives	
4.	Language and Craft	**Seamus Heaney,** "Trout" (Poetry)
5.	Focus on the Writer	

Reading Focus

1. Active readers annotate the text, building their understanding by paying attention to the language and ideas.

2. Experiences are remembered as stories. But these stories can be presented in many forms depending on the effect an author wants to create.

3. Look at a reading from several angles. Think about how changing the point of view changes the effect that the text has on a reader.

4. Active reading requires paying close attention to how the words and structure of a text go together.

5. Knowing about a writer's life can help you understand his or her work. Use insights about a writer to help you read.

Writing Focus

1. Summarize a poem, including specific examples from the text.
2. After listing the events in a poem, rewrite the poem as a news story.
3. Describe what happened in a poem from a different point of view.
4. Complete a double-entry log about the comparisons in a poem.
5. Interpret a poem in this cluster from a new angle, explaining how your understanding of the work has evolved.

One Interactions with the Text

Critical Reading

FOCUS

From *How to Mark a Book* by Mortimer J. Adler:

"Full ownership of a book comes only when you have made it a part of yourself, and the best way to make yourself a part of it is by writing in it."

BACKGROUND

Experienced readers instinctively "read between the lines." This lesson demonstrates how "writing between the lines" makes reading an active experience. Challenging texts like the poetry of Seamus Heaney, which are rich in ideas and beauty, require the most active reading we can manage.

➤ Seamus Heaney was born on a farm west of Belfast in Northern Ireland in 1939. In 1995 he won the Nobel Prize for Literature. If we assume that the speaker in "Digging" is Heaney, we believe that he compares his work as a writer with the digging of his father and grandfather in turf and potato fields. The first stanza describes the poet, pen in hand, ready to write: "The squat pen rests; snug as a gun." The middle stanzas recall scenes from the narrator's youth when he watched men cut turf. In the final lines of the poem the writer reflects on how, though he has "no spade to follow men like them," he will take up the pen in his hand and "dig with it."

➤ In "Blackberry-Picking" Heaney again uses vivid sensory images to describe a bittersweet memory. The first stanza details the heady pleasure of berry picking and the speaker's insatiable hunger for the fruit. In the second stanza, he describes the inevitable change which occurs soon afterwards: "The fruit fermented, the sweet flesh would turn sour. / I always felt like crying. It wasn't fair." The poem records a lesson in the mutability of life.

FOR DISCUSSION AND REFLECTION

➤ Draw students' attention to the way the annotations of "Digging" demonstrate one reader's emerging understanding of the poem. Ask students to share their annotations of "Blackberry-Picking" with a partner to see what they can tell about their classmate's reading of the poem.

➤ In "Digging," what is the narrator's attitude toward the memories he recalls? (Students should note admiration for his forebearers' achievements and fear that he may not be able to achieve as much. All the memories are wistful.)

Writing

QUICK ASSESS

Do students' summaries:

✔ make use of the details they identified in their annotations?

✔ demonstrate an appreciation for sensory details?

✔ reflect an awareness of the author's stance in the poem?

As students prepare to write a brief summary of "Blackberry-Picking," draw attention to Heaney's use of sensory details to make a memory live again for the reader. Make a list of specific words and phrases from the poem for possible use in their summaries.

READING AND WRITING EXTENSIONS

➤ Have students compare "Blackberry-Picking" with Gerard Manley Hopkins's "Spring and Fall: To a Young Child" ("Margaret, are you grieving / Over Goldengrove unleaving?").

➤ Invite students to write a poem of their own describing a bittersweet memory. Like the poems of Seamus Heaney and Gerard Manley Hopkins, students' poems should include an underlying observation or message.

Two Story Connections

Critical Reading

FOCUS
From *The Call of Stories* by Robert Coles:

"Their story, yours, mine—it's what we all carry with us on this trip we take, and we owe it to each other to respect our stories and learn from them."

BACKGROUND

"Mid-Term Break" contains within it a story about the death of the narrator's four-year-old brother. In order to understand the details of this story, a reader must probe the lines of the text for information. Unlike a newspaper story where the events are listed in order of importance, a poem purposely changes events to create an effect. Many students find this frustrating, but by guiding them through the details of Heaney's story, you can help students see how a poem communicates much more than the bare facts. A rich poem like Heaney's allows active readers to experience the story through the speaker's thoughts and perceptions.

➤ The title of the poem is ironic. The narrator is called away from school for the funeral of his younger brother who has been hit by a car: "Wearing a poppy bruise on his left temple . . . . / No gaudy scars, the bumper knocked him clear." This is the opposite of the vacation one expects from a "Mid-Term Break."

FOR DISCUSSION AND REFLECTION

➤ What does the fact that he was sitting in the college sick bay suggest? (The narrator has been told of the death by an administrator and awaits retrieval to attend the funeral. Perhaps he did not feel like attending class after hearing the news.)

➤ How might the state of his parents ("my father crying— / He had always taken funerals in his stride—" and "my mother held my hand / In hers and coughed out angry tearless sighs") influence the narrator's own outward response? (He may be the one they will lean on now and trust to be strong.)

➤ How is the line "I saw him / For the first time in six weeks" painfully ironic? (The last time the narrator saw him, the boy was alive.)

Writing

QUICK ASSESS
Do students' articles:

✓ include the events they identified in order of their importance?

✓ provide information about who, what, where, when, and why?

After students have written their articles, have a few read theirs aloud. On the board identify how the writers have included the who, what, where, when, and why. When sharing the differences they have observed between the story poem and the news story, some students may insist that they much prefer a journalistic account of an event. This is an honest response. As literature teachers, we can only hope that more experience with poetry will cause them to reconsider.

READING AND WRITING EXTENSIONS

➤ Have students write a short account of a moment in elementary school when they were deeply embarrassed. Be sure to include the five Ws. Then invite students to turn what they have written into a story poem.

➤ On a lighter note, have students read "Headphone Harold" from Shel Silverstein's *Falling Up* and discuss this story poem's didactic message: the dangers of walking on train tracks while plugged in to a Walkman.

Three Shifting Perspectives

Critical Reading

FOCUS

Point of view is the physical, cultural, temporal, and emotional stance from which we view the world.

BACKGROUND

Just as where you stand to view a landscape influences what you see, so a character's point of view influences what he or she sees and feels. Seamus Heaney's poem "Mid-Term Break" is told from the point of view of a young student, confused by the loss of his younger brother and unsure of how he should feel. Imagining how other characters in this poem might see events opens up interpretive possibilities for readers.

➤ Remind students that point of view is the vantage point from which a story is presented. Help them to understand why it matters who tells a story by having them pose "What if" questions: What if the porch scene were described by a neighbor or the ambulance driver? What if the body were described by a doctor? Discuss together how changing perspectives can deepen their understanding of what they read.

FOR DISCUSSION AND REFLECTION

➤ How does the narrator's age and six-week absence from his family possibly influence his point of view? (He is at a distance from them, both physically and intellectually.)

➤ What evidence in the poem do you have of the father's and mother's points of view? ("my father crying," "my mother . . . coughed out angry tearless sighs")

Writing

QUICK ASSESS

Do students' descriptions:

✓ demonstrate how shifting points of view can change the nature of a story?

✓ use a neighbor's perspective?

Students are asked to shift the point of view of this story to a neighbor who is being interviewed by a newspaper reporter for a story about the accident. Encourage them to think about how emotional the neighbor's story might be and to reflect on how changes in the point of view alter the effect that the text has on the reader.

READING AND WRITING EXTENSIONS

➤ Ask students to write three diary entries describing the day the diarist met the person of his or her dreams: one by a giggly teenage girl, a second by a 40-year-old stamp collector who lives with his mother, a third by an 85-year-old widower living in a retirement village. Have them contrast their entries in light of the various perspectives.

➤ Read Alfred Lord Tennyson's "The Eagle" to your students and discuss how the bird's point of view affects the reader's perspective on sky ("the azure world") and water ("wrinkled sea").

Four Language and Craft

Critical Reading

FOCUS

A metaphor is a figure of speech in which a writer implies similarities between apparently unlike things.

For instance, Seamus Heaney's trout is "a fat gun-barrel."

BACKGROUND

In order to appreciate the comparisons Seamus Heaney makes in his poem "Trout," students may need to be provided with some specific information about this particular breed of fish. Many will probably only have ever seen a trout on ice.

➤ *The Oxford English Dictonary* describes trout as "a freshwater fish of the genus *Salmo*, the common trout, inhabiting most rivers and lakes in the temperate or colder parts of the northern hemisphere; it is distinguished by numerous spots of red and black on its side and head and is greatly valued as a sporting fish and on account of its edible quality."

➤ In "Trout," Seamus Heaney uses figurative language to communicate to readers what he has observed and imagined regarding the life of a trout. Many of the metaphors and similes describe the fish in motion: "slips like butter down / the throat of the river," "fired from the shallows / white belly reporting," "darts like a tracer— / bullet."

FOR DISCUSSION AND REFLECTION

➤ Read students the dictionary definition of a trout and ask them to articulate the differences between this kind of a description of a trout and the one Heaney provides in his poem. (The fish in the dictionary definition feels dead while Heaney's lives and breathes.)

➤ Is the figurative language of poets as precise as the language used by those who write dictionaries? Would you be able to identify a trout from the poem? Discuss the different purposes of these two kinds of language. (Dictionaries define words for a reader. Heaney's poem allows readers imaginatively to participate in the experience of a trout and deepens our understanding of the word.)

Writing

QUICK ASSESS

Do students' logs:

✔ recognize examples of figurative language?

✔ explain the implications of the comparisons they noted?

Write samples of what students have written in their double-entry logs on the board. Invite discussion of possible interpretations of Heaney's description of the trout. Allow students who have had difficulty explaining the figurative language they found to copy into their log what others have suggested or to revise their initial interpretations.

READING AND WRITING EXTENSIONS

➤ Ask students to choose an animal whose habits and behavior they know well and create a list of five similes and five metaphors describing this animal in action. Based upon this list, have them compose a poem of their own.

➤ *Poetry Like Bread* is a collection of poetry edited by Martin Espada. Ask students to speculate why an editor might choose this simile for an anthology. What is he suggesting about readers? (Perhaps that we need the nourishment of poetry as much as we need bread.)

Five Focus on the Writer

Critical Reading

FOCUS

Seamus Heaney feels that generations of rural ancestors — who, while not illiterate, were not literary either — are asserting themselves within him.

BACKGROUND

Reading what others have written about an author's work and then reevaluating the work in terms of this new information is a common beginning for literary scholarship. This lesson exposes students to common types of secondary sources in literature study: biographical information and literary interpretation. As beginners in the field, students often ascribe every occurrence in a writer's body of work that appears in the first person as autobiographical. Reminding students of what they learned earlier about shifting perspectives should help to clarify how an author's point of view may shift even when describing events in his or her own life, depending upon the effects the poet wants to achieve.

FOR DISCUSSION AND REFLECTION

➤ How does the biographical information in the first excerpt — knowing that the family "crowded together in the three rooms . . . and lived a kind of den-life which was more or less emotionally and intellectually proofed against the outside world" — influence your reading of "Mid-Term Break"? (Answers will vary.)

➤ Can a reader necessarily equate details from writers' poetry with details from their lives? (Alert students to the danger of such an assumption. Artists often use their lives in their art but do not necessarily reproduce it.)

➤ How does the information provided in the second excerpt regarding Heaney's preference for the solitary life help you to reflect upon the author's stance in both "Digging" and "Trout"? (Both fishing and writing are quiet acts most often performed alone.)

Writing

QUICK ASSESS

Do students' paragraphs:

✓ make insightful connections between the information about Heaney and the poetry they have read?

✓ interpret a poem from a new angle?

Students are asked to interpret one of Seamus Heaney's poems from an angle of literacy not previously explored. As a prewriting activity, discuss some of the notes they made about the four quotations. Help them to be specific in noting connections among the critical and biographical passages and the poems.

READING AND WRITING EXTENSIONS

➤ Invite students to become literary detectives and search the Internet for additional information about Seamus Heaney. They may report their findings either in writing for a bulletin board on Heaney or orally to the class.

➤ Have students compile a list of questions that they would like to ask Seamus Heaney if he were to visit their class tomorrow.

THE LESSONS STORIES TEACH

U n i t   O v e r v i e w

"The Lessons Stories Teach" explores how authors use patterns of action and symbols to convey meaning. Students will read and respond to poems, short stories, and an excerpt from an essay on symbolic language to help them understand the nature of symbols.

L i t e r a t u r e   F o c u s

	Lesson	Literature
1.	Patterns in Stories	**Ovid,** "The Story of Midas" from *The Metamorphoses* (Poetry)
2.	Symbolic Meaning	**Erich Fromm,** from "The Nature of Symbolic Language" (Nonfiction)
		Andrei Voznesensky, "First Frost" (Poetry)
3.	Understanding New Symbols	**Leslie Marmon Silko,** from "The Man to Send Rain Clouds" (Short Story)
4.	Familiar Symbols in Unfamiliar Places	**Ray Bradbury,** "December 2001: The Green Morning" (Short Story)
5.	A Network of Symbols in Story	

R e a d i n g   F o c u s

1. Examining the patterns of action and their significance helps you understand the meaning of a story.
2. Symbols are used to show the connections between the physical world (sensory) and the world of the mind (emotional and intellectual).
3. Noticing details at the literal level, connecting them to symbols that are familiar, and making inferences about their possible meaning can help you understand the use of symbols.
4. Writers use familiar symbols as a way of grounding readers in reality while challenging them to understand complex ideas.
5. Examine the symbols used in a story to determine how they contribute to the meaning of the story.

W r i t i n g   F o c u s

1. Write a short story, using a familiar pattern to teach a lesson.
2. Explain how the sensory details in a poem connect to the title.
3. Write a short essay about the symbols in a story.
4. Create a series of drawings depicting a character's actions.
5. Write a continuation of a story.

One Patterns in Stories

Critical Reading

FOCUS

An allegory is a symbolic fictional narrative that conveys a secondary meaning not explicitly set forth in the story.

BACKGROUND

The story of King Midas and his touch of gold has entered common usage. We might say of a successful businessman that "everything he touches turns to gold." Midas Muffler shops use golden folders for their receipts. What is sometimes forgotten is the lesson this story was intended to teach: that greed will result in self-destruction.

➤ After having hospitably entertained a companion of Bacchus when the man had lost his way, King Midas is granted one wish. The foolish and greedy king chooses that "whatever I touch may turn to gold." At first this seems a great boon, but when the very meat Midas attempts to eat becomes gold in his mouth, he asks to be relieved of the gift. Midas is ordered to wash in a river whose sands thereafter contained gold.

➤ You may want to review with students certain vocabulary words (judicious, ruinous, ingots, and imbued). Ask students to try and figure out the words' meanings from context before providing them with definitions.

➤ There are also mythological references that may need explaining. For example, the Hesperides is home to the Daughters of Evening, nymphs who guard a tree which produces golden apples. Ceres is goddess of the earth's fertility; thus bread is a "gift of Ceres." The word "cereal" is derived from her name.

FOR DISCUSSION AND REFLECTION

➤ Why are stories effective vehicles for teaching us lessons about life? (Though we recoil from didactic messages that tell us "do this" or "don't do that," most everyone loves a good story.)

➤ How does a familiarity with classical mythology assist your reading of literature? (Many writers use references from mythology in contemporary stories.)

Writing

QUICK ASSESS

Do students' stories:

✓ reproduce the patterns in the King Midas story?

✓ teach a lesson?

Students are asked to write an updated version of the Midas story. Before students begin to write their own allegory, list possible misguided wishes that one might make: sunshine every day, no school ever, the fastest car in the world.

READING AND WRITING EXTENSIONS

➤ *Aesop's Fables* are some of the best-known allegorical stories in literature. Read one of these aloud to the class (use the original versions rather than a children's book retellings of the stories) and ask students to determine what they feel are the lessons to be learned. Students are likely to be familiar with "Crying 'Wolf'," "The Hare and the Tortoise," and "The Country Mouse and the Town Mouse."

➤ Write an imaginary dialogue between King Midas and his own daughter (who in some versions of this myth was also temporarily turned to gold when he went to embrace her). What advice would he want to give her?

Two Symbolic Meaning

Critical Reading

A symbol is something that stands for something else, not by exact resemblance but by suggestion.

BACKGROUND

The King Midas story in Lesson One uses gold as a symbol of greed. Writers often use material objects to represent an abstract idea or quality in this manner. While students may occasionally accuse their English teachers of being "symbol-minded," in fact, most complex literature is rich in symbols.

➤ Erich Fromm explains how the symbol of fire resonates for sensitive readers. He describes the connections between the physical properties of fire and the ideas and qualities that the symbol "fire" inspires: energy, warmth, destruction, light.

➤ In the poem "First Frost," by Andrei Voznesensky, frost is used as a symbol for the girl's emotional state. Just as frost is a warning of colder days to come, so the phone message and the way it has made her feel are precursors to future loss and pain.

FOR DISCUSSION AND REFLECTION

➤ What kinds of words are most often used symbolically? (Before students create clusters of their own symbol with its associative meanings, make a list on the board of possible words that would work for this exercise: water, air, green, sugar, breath, rock, tree, iron, ice, mirror.)

➤ In "First Frost," what does the detail that the girl is freezing "in her flimsy coat" suggest about her state of mind? (She is unprepared for the emotional chill that is coming her way.)

➤ What does the detail that she is wearing "Glass beads in her ears" suggest about her? (She is probably young, relatively poor, and inexperienced in the ways of love. No one has yet given her diamonds. Glass beads are also very like tears.)

Writing

QUICK ASSESS

Do students' explanations:

✔ recognize symbolic language in the poem?

✔ connect the sensory details to the meaning of the title?

Before students write their explanations of how the title "First Frost" links to the sensory details in the poem, ask them to articulate why writers choose to employ symbols rather than simply describe emotions. Consider why abstractions do not communicate meaning to readers nearly as well as concrete images and symbols.

READING AND WRITING EXTENSIONS

➤ Ask students to write an imaginary dialogue between the girl in the telephone booth and the person at the other end of the line. Be sure their closing remarks reflect the emotional content of the poem's final stanza.

➤ Have students rehearse readings of these scripts and perform a few dialogues for the whole class.

Three Understanding New Symbols

Critical Reading

FOCUS

Leslie Marmon Silko on meanings in stories:

"Inside the old stories told among tribal people are the same kind of valuable lessons about human behavior that we all still need."

BACKGROUND

Leslie Marmon Silko grew up on the Laguna Pueblo Reservation where members of her family had lived for generations and where she learned the traditional stories and legends of her people. Silko's first published book was *Laguna Woman* (1974), a collection of poems which draws richly from her tribal ancestry. Her much-acclaimed novel *Ceremony* (1977) is the story of a Native American of mixed ancestry who returns after fighting in the Second World War to his Laguna reservation to be healed.

➤ In "The Man to Send Rain Clouds," many of the symbols Silko employs are unfamiliar to readers from outside her culture. This lesson is designed to help students see that unfamiliar symbols need not shut them out of a story. As students begin to speculate on likely connections and meanings for symbols they do not at first recognize, they come to understand the universal nature of symbols.

FOR DISCUSSION AND REFLECTION

➤ How do you know that Ken and Leon's actions, though unfamiliar to your experience, have meaning? (They are performed with great care and purpose. They have not been improvised on the spot. These are rituals intended to "Send us rain clouds, Grandfather.")

➤ What does Ken and Leon's exchange with Father Paul suggest about their relationship with the priest? (Though amiable, he clearly does not understand their tribal rituals. Ken and Leon choose not to explain; Father Paul remains clueless. Readers who wait for explanation rather that working to make symbolic connections on their own may similarly have difficulty understanding Native American literature.)

Writing

QUICK ASSESS

Do students' essays:

✔ explain the meaning of the story's symbols?

✔ describe inferences they made about the poem's details?

Students are asked to write a short essay describing what they think the symbols in the excerpt from "The Man to Send Rain Clouds" mean. Remind students that their interpretations may not be identical to those of someone from the Laguna culture.

READING AND WRITING EXTENSIONS

➤ In her book *Storyteller*, Leslie Marmon Silko re-creates ancient stories by weaving through them stories from her own family. The text includes poetry, prose, and photographs. Read passages to students and see if they can apply their new-found skill with unfamiliar symbols.

➤ Have students write a story incorporating symbols that are rich in meaning for them but that could be difficult for someone unfamiliar with their culture to understand.

Four Familiar Symbols in Unfamiliar Places

Critical Reading

FOCUS

Always intrigued by the possibilities of the future, Ray Bradbury expresses an optimism about the fate of our world.

BACKGROUND

Though "December 2001: The Green Morning" is set in the future and in a land far away, Bradbury's symbols are familiar. He uses air, breath, water, seeds, fire, earth, and sun on Mars almost exactly as another writer might use them on Earth. Science fiction is sometimes considered an escape from reality, but literary scholar Russell Kirk has called Bradbury's stories, "not an escape from reality but windows looking upon enduring reality, the reality of truth glimpsed through wonder."

➤ When, soon after his arrival, the story's hero Benjamin Driscoll faints, a doctor explains that "the air's pretty thin. Some can't take it. I think you'll have to go back to earth." Benjamin refuses to leave and devises a plan to bring more oxygen to the Martian atmosphere. Like Johnny Appleseed, he decides to plant trees.

➤ Students may need to be reminded how photosynthesis works in order to make the connection between more trees and increased oxygen. Using energy from sunlight, leaf cells turn carbon dioxide and water into food. One of the main byproducts of photosynthesis is oxygen.

FOR DISCUSSION AND REFLECTION

➤ How does Benjamin Driscoll's weakness (his sensitivity to the thin air) become the motive behind his actions? (In the process of making the planet habitable for himself, he improves the quality of life there for everyone.)

➤ Is Driscoll a hero? (Responses may vary) How is he similar to other heroes from mythology and legend: Odysseus, Beowulf, Achilles, Hercules, Roland, Hector? What qualities do they all share? (Possible answers include undaunted courage, determination, and seemingly inexhaustible energy.)

Writing

QUICK ASSESS

Do students' drawings:

✓ depict key actions in the story, including a prediction about what will happen next?

✓ reflect the hero's symbolic significance?

Students are asked to explore their understanding of Benjamin Driscoll as a symbol through a series of drawings depicting the steps he takes on his heroic journey. Remind them that a hero is a legendary figure usually endowed with great strength or ability. A hero accepts challenges and sometimes even courts disaster.

READING AND WRITING EXTENSIONS

➤ Have students research Johnny Appleseed in the library or on the Internet and report back to the class on how his accomplishments are similar to Driscoll's. Discuss how Bradbury has used readers' knowledge of this traditional story to enrich his own story.

➤ Invite students to write a science fiction story of their own in which their hero solves a problem through undaunted courage, determination, and seemingly inexhaustible energy.

Five A Network of Symbols in Story

Critical Reading

FOCUS

Some writers use a network of symbols to convey meaning.

BACKGROUND

Ray Bradbury's writing often elicits strong reactions from readers. His many works (including *The Martian Chronicles*, *The Illustrated Man*, *Dandelion Wine*, and *Something Wicked This Way Comes*) are always informed by ethics. According to editor James Person, Bradbury's ethics "bespeak his belief that human beings are more than the flies of summer; that they are in fact made for knowing beauty, truth and eternity; and that each movement toward political centralization, materialism and expediency endangers all that makes life fulfilling and worthwhile, rendering man little more than a trousered ape."

FOR DISCUSSION AND REFLECTION

➤ How do you think life will change for Driscoll and the colonists now that "five thousand new trees have climbed up into the yellow sun"? (Answers will vary.)

➤ What is the lesson that this story has to tell readers about colonization and development on other planets? (As man travels to other worlds, he would do well to bring, along with the things he has learned about science, the stories that he knows—for example, Johnny Appleseed. In order for man to thrive in a new environment, he must have a symbolic connection to the old.)

➤ How has Bradbury used a network of symbols to achieve his fictional purposes? (The use of familiar symbols helps the reader to reflect on how in the future and in unfamiliar places man will still rely on the same inner resources in order to survive.)

Writing

QUICK ASSESS

Do students' endings:

✔ build on the story's meaning?

✔ use symbols that the author introduced?

Students are asked to take their speculations about what might happen next in Bradbury's story and to write a continuation. Remind them to incorporate the symbols that Bradbury has used as well as others that will enrich the symbolic meaning of the story. Invite students to explore the ramifications of such a change as Driscoll has created in atmosphere.

READING AND WRITING EXTENSIONS

➤ Have students write a series of diary entries for Benjamin Driscoll, beginning with his arrival on the airless planet and ending with this day of triumph.

➤ Whenever the budget gets tight, our government considers cutting funds for space exploration. Have students write a letter to the editor expressing their views on whether or not the United States should continue to spend tax dollars on the space program.

HEROES AND HEROINES

U n i t   O v e r v i e w

In this unit students will focus on what our choices of heroes and heroines reveal about ourselves and our culture. By reading poetry, song lyrics, and an essay, students will explore variations in the concept of heroism and learn to challenge, question, and compare heroic ideals.

L i t e r a t u r e   F o c u s

	Lesson	Literature
1.	Who Is a Hero?	from *Beowulf* (Poetry)
2.	Who Is a Heroine?	**Homer,** from *The Odyssey* (Poetry)
		John Lennon and Paul McCartney, "Lady Madonna" (Song)
3.	Models for Living	**Alice Walker,** "A Name Is Sometimes An Ancestor Saying HI, I'm With You" (Nonfiction)
4.	Are Heroes Always Admirable?	**Louise Erdrich,** "Dear John Wayne" (Poetry)
5.	Who Are My Heroes or Heroines?	**Robert Hayden,** "Frederick Douglass" (Poetry)

R e a d i n g   F o c u s

1. Examining heroic characters helps us understand how the concept of heroism has varied in different time periods and places.
2. Heroines in literature are symbolic of the qualities of character that were admired in women in different time periods and places.
3. Heroes and heroines are a major influence for good in people's lives, providing examples of action, commitment, and belief.
4. Writers not only create characterizations of heroes and heroines, but also question or challenge the representations that have been made by others.
5. Often the heroes or heroines that you identify with are those that most nearly represent your own values and experiences.

W r i t i n g   F o c u s

1. Write a speech in which a modern hero tells a revealing story.
2. Create a dialogue between two heroines discussing the qualities they admire in women.
3. Write an essay about someone who has been a model of conduct for you.
4. Use a model to write a poem that questions the admirable qualities of a hero or heroine.
5. Compose a tribute to a personal hero or heroine as a poem or short essay.

One Who Is a Hero?

Critical Reading

FOCUS

From *The Hero with a Thousand Faces* by Joseph Campbell:

"The mythological hero, setting forth from his commonday hut or castle, is lured, carried away, or else voluntarily proceeds, to the threshold of adventure."

BACKGROUND

In this lesson, students are asked to reflect upon the concept of the hero. As they list the names of men who qualify for the exalted title and discuss with classmates why they have chosen these particular individuals, certain common characteristics will emerge. These qualities are a working definition of "hero" upon which future lessons will build.

➤ The passage from *Beowulf* that students are asked to read takes place soon after Beowulf has arrived at Herot, King Hrothgar's renowned meadhall. Beowulf has heard that Hrothgar is plagued by the monster Grendel and has come to save the day. Unferth, Hrothgar's greatest warrior, is affronted by the appearance of the hero and, slightly drunk, belittles Beowulf's heroic deeds. The excerpt is Beowulf's angry reply to Unferth.

➤ No more apt example of a larger than life hero exists in literature. Beowulf tells Unferth that, armed with an iron sword and covered in chain mail — remember, no steel back then — he swam in the frozen sea for five days and five nights killing nine huge monsters. It is hard to argue with Beowulf's claim that, "Neither he nor you can match me - and I mean / No boast, have announced no more than I know / To be true."

FOR DISCUSSION AND REFLECTION

➤ Ask students to identify the tone of Beowulf's speech. (Some may see this as distasteful boasting on the part of the hero, but from Beowulf's point of view he is simply describing what happened. He is supremely confident, utterly self-assured, and comfortable in the role of a hero. Modesty is not one of the defining characteristics of the hero.)

➤ Invite students to think about other characters from literature or film that appear larger than life and to compare these heroes with Beowulf. (Possible responses include Indiana Jones, James Bond, Superman, and Hercules.)

Writing

QUICK ASSESS

Do students' speeches:

✔ reveal a range of heroic qualities and deeds?

✔ have the hero tell a boastful story similar to Beowulf's?

Before students begin to write speeches for one of their heroes, have them share their lists of modern heroes and look closely at the structure of Beowulf's speech. He begins with an insult to Unferth and then proceeds to set the record straight. The rest of what follows is a detailed description of his exploits in the sea.

READING AND WRITING EXTENSIONS

➤ John Gardner has rewritten Beowulf's story from the point of view of the monster. His contemporary novel *Grendel* offers a very different take on the hero. Read the last chapter of the book to students aloud and ask them to write what Grendel's definition of a hero would be.

➤ Heroes often have songs written about their glorious deeds. Ask students to choose a hero and write a song in praise of him.

Two Who Is a Heroine?

Critical Reading

FOCUS

From *The Hero with a Thousand Faces* by Joseph Campbell:

"Woman, in the picture language of mythology, represents the totality of what can be known. The hero is the one who comes to know. As he progresses in the slow initiation which is life, the form of the goddess undergoes for him a series of transfigurations: she can never be greater than himself, though she can always promise more than he is yet capable of comprehending."

BACKGROUND

As students shift perspectives and examine the question "Who is a heroine?" certain difficulties may surface. The role of a woman in traditional literature and mythology has not been that of the hero.

➤ In the passage from *The Odyssey*, Circe provides the hero Odysseus with advice about how to get around the monsters and other obstacles which stand in the way of his return to Ithaca. She had intended to turn Odysseus and his men into swine, but with a magic potion from another god, the hero overpowered Circe, thus earning her assistance.

➤ The lyrics of "Lady Madonna" portray a very different heroine. In this instance, the woman whose name is reminiscent of Mary, the mother of Jesus, is a heroine by virtue of her suffering. Despite overwhelmingly difficult circumstances and more children than she seems to know what to do with, Lady Madonna survives.

FOR DISCUSSION AND REFLECTION

➤ Ask students if they can think of examples in modern literature or film where women have been cast in the role of a heroine? (Responses might include Janie Walker in Zora Neale Hurston's *Their Eyes Were Watching God*, Rayona in Michael Dorris's *Yellow Raft in Blue Water*, and Offred in Margaret Atwood's *The Handmaid's Tale*.)

➤ What might account for the different roles women are beginning to play in stories? (Responses will vary.)

Writing

QUICK ASSESS

Do students' dialogues:

✓ explain the general qualities in women that each speaker admires?

✓ reflect an understanding of differences between the speakers' personalities, values, and speech patterns?

In order to write a dialogue between Circe and Lady Madonna, students may first need to talk about these two women's relationship with the men in their lives. Help them see how different the speech patterns of these two women would be and speculate on what different tones of voice they might use. To spark creativity, have two students "perform" a brief conversation you have written.

READING AND WRITING EXTENSIONS

➤ Ask students to bring to class song lyrics that portray women as heroines. As they listen to these songs, have students identify heroic qualities, such as loyalty, strength, determination, fearlessness, or power.

➤ Read Eudora Welty's short story "Circe" and discuss how the story from *The Odyssey* changes when told from the point of view of Circe.

Three Models for Living

Critical Reading

FOCUS

Sojourner Truth took her name because she planned to journey from place to place declaring the truth to whoever would listen as well as to those who would not:

"I could work as much, and eat as much as man—when I could get it—and bear the lash as well! And ain't I a woman? I have borne children and seen most of them sold into slavery, and when I cried out with a mother's grief, none but Jesus heard me. And ain't I a woman?"

BACKGROUND

Born in 1944 in Eaton, Georgia, to sharecropper parents, Alice Walker has become one of the best-known writers in America. In her essay "A Name Is Sometimes An Ancestor Saying HI, I'm With You," Walker explains how Sojourner Truth has been a model for Walker's life.

➤ Sojourner Truth's given name was Isabella Bomefree. She was born a slave and married a fellow slave at the age of 14. Truth eventually gained her freedom in her late 20s and, as a deeply religious person, answered an evangelical calling. In 1843 she felt called by God to change her name to Sojourner Truth to reflect her mission as an evangelical wanderer and truth teller. A tireless worker for the abolition of slavery and the rights of women, Sojourner Truth was described by Frederick Douglass as a "strange compound of wit and wisdom, of wild enthusiasm, and flint-like common sense." Walker says that she has drawn strength from Sojourner Truth and found in her life, lessons for herself: "Every experience that roused her passion against injustice in her lifetime shines from my eyes."

FOR DISCUSSION AND REFLECTION

➤ Ask students to discuss if they need heroes and heroines to model ways of living. (Responses will vary.)

➤ How does the example of Sojourner Truth and Alice Walker demonstrate that these models for living need not be a blueprint for behavior but rather an inspiration? (Responses will vary.)

Writing

QUICK ASSESS

Do students' essays:

✓ use Walker's essay as a model?

✓ explain how someone has served as a model of conduct for them?

Remind students that they need not choose only from famous people for their essay. The individual who was a model of conduct for them might have been a coach, a relative, a sports hero, or a character in a story they once read.

READING AND WRITING EXTENSIONS

➤ Writing about her admiration for her mother in her essay, "In Search of Our Mothers' Gardens," Alice Walker talks about watching her mother at the end of a day of back-breaking physical labor on someone else's farm return home only to walk the long distance to their well to get water for her garden. Walker watched her design that garden, putting tall plants at the back and planting so as to have something in bloom from early spring until the end of summer. While not knowing what she was seeing at the time, the adult Walker names her mother an artist full of dedication, with a keen sense of design and balance, and a tough conviction that life without beauty is unbearable. Have students debate whether beauty is a necessity or a luxury.

➤ Ask students to write about how the creation of this garden could be seen as another model for Walker's life as a writer.

Four Are Heroes Always Admirable?

Critical Reading

BACKGROUND

Louise Erdrich is a member of the Turtle Mountain Reservation in North Dakota. Her mother is French Ojibwe and her father German American. While she was growing up, her parents worked at the Bureau of Indian Affairs School in Wahpeton, North Dakota.

➤ Her poem "Dear John Wayne" is a critique of the traditional American cowboy hero. The setting for the poem is a drive-in movie theater on a hot summer night. The "we" in the poem are a group of young Native Americans lounging "on the hood of the Pontiac" under the stars "beneath the sign of the bear." They are watching a film where Indians are cast as savages, "swarming down on the settlers / who die beautifully."

➤ As the credits roll, the laughing young people get back into the car, "speechless and small . . . . We are back in ourselves." Erdrich suggests that the destruction begun by John Wayne (metaphorically, as a symbolic hero of the Westward movement) continues to play itself out in the lives of these moviegoers: "Come on, boys, we've got them / where we want them, drunk, running. / They will give us what we want, what we need." But what happens when John Wayne needs everything the Indians have? What if nothing is left but the heart?

FOR DISCUSSION AND REFLECTION

➤ Ask students to speculate as to why John Wayne might become a focus of criticism. What does he represent? (Responses will vary.)

➤ What other traditional American heroes' behavior has been called into question by Native Americans? (Possible responses include Christopher Columbus, John Smith, General Custer, the Pilgrims.) By African Americans? (Possible responses include George Washington and Thomas Jefferson.)

➤ Have students choose a line in the poem that struck them as the strongest critique.

Writing

Do a model of the poetry writing assignment with students. Then let them begin their own poems using Erdrich's two-part structure.

READING AND WRITING EXTENSIONS

➤ In Gerald Vizenor's *The Heirs of Columbus*, the theme of cultural aggression is turned on its head. Stone Columbus, crossblood trickster and modern namesake of the explorer, is born on a reservation and secures a fortune on a bingo barge. In a madcap series of events, the heirs of Columbus reclaim their misrepresented heritage. Read and discuss the opening passage.

➤ Read from Garry Wills's book *John Wayne's America* and discuss how it is possible that many decades after his death many Americans still chose John Wayne as their favorite actor.

Five Who Are My Heroes or Heroines?

Critical Reading

FOCUS

Our choice of heroes says a great deal about what we value in the world and in ourselves.

BACKGROUND

Born a slave, Frederick Douglass taught himself to read, escaped bondage, and emerged as one of the nineteenth century's most eloquent orators and writers. His autobiographies, beginning with the *Narrative of the Life of Frederick Douglass* (1845), galvanized the antislavery movement in the United States.

Robert Hayden's poem is a tribute to the man, celebrating not only Douglass's achievements during his lifetime but also the inspiration Douglass has been: "Oh, not with statues' rhetoric, / not with legends and poems and wreaths of bronze alone, / but with the lives grown out of his life."

In *Frederick Douglass*, biographer William S. McFeely paints a vivid picture of the man's heroic qualities: "Exhilarated by the 1866 convention, Douglass wanted a place in the constructing of his new America. There was a world of work to do, and he was ready. As a citizen who had long championed full citizenship for his fellow black Americans, he was convinced that what they most needed was the vote. To achieve that goal the constitution he revered needed only an amendment. He was confident that he was the man in America who could best exemplify, in his person, the soundness of enfranchising his people." (p. 253)

FOR DISCUSSION AND REFLECTION

➤ Ask students to compare Robert Hayden's praise for Frederick Douglass with Alice Walker's praise for Sojourner Truth. Do you think Douglass is a model for Hayden the way Sojourner Truth is for Walker? (Answers will vary.)

➤ Compare what the paragraph from Douglass's biography suggests about the hero's opinion of himself with Beowulf's speech in Lesson One. (Answers may focus on issues of self-confidence.)

Writing

QUICK ASSESS

Do students' tributes:

✔ explain why they value this person as well as identify specific admirable qualities?

✔ demonstrate an appreciation of the structure used by Walker and Hayden?

A tribute is a gift rendered as acknowledgment of affection or esteem. As students write their tribute to a personal hero, be sure they include not only details from the hero's life but also an explanation of why they value what this man or woman has achieved.

READING AND WRITING EXTENSIONS

➤ In his "I Have a Dream" speech, Martin Luther King looked forward to a day when his children would be judged not for the color of their skin but for the content of their character. Ask students if they think this day has come. Suggest that they research how the country is faring in terms of racial equality and share their findings with the class.

➤ Have students research the life of Frederick Douglass and then share the information they have found.

NEW WAYS OF SEEING AND KNOWING

U n i t   O v e r v i e w

In this unit, students are invited to explore several strategies for understanding an author's meaning. By reading and responding to details in the work of William Least Heat Moon, Rachel Carson, Edward Abbey, and Sylvia Plath, students will develop their abilities to comprehend a text at three levels – literally, interpretively, and critically.

L i t e r a t u r e   F o c u s

	Lesson	Literature
1.	Seeing the Details	**William Least Heat Moon,** from *Blue Highways*: *A Journey Into America* (Nonfiction)
2.	Seeing the Literal Meaning	**Rachel Carson,** from "The Marginal World" (Nonfiction)
3.	Observing and Interpreting	**Edward Abbey,** from "Freedom and Wilderness" (Nonfiction)
4.	Looking Beneath the Surface	**Sylvia Plath,** "Mushrooms" (Poetry)
5.	Comprehending Critically	**William Least Heat Moon,** from *Blue Highways*: *A Journey Into America* (Nonfiction)

R e a d i n g   F o c u s

1. In reading, as in traveling, it is important to pay attention to the details.
2. Using your mind's eye—envisioning the scene an author describes—as you read is a way to improve your comprehension of the details and the literal meaning.
3. Writers give meaning to their work by the details they choose to include. Readers need to read carefully to interpret the details.
4. Looking beneath the surface of a text will reveal additional insights and meanings.
5. When you read, you apply the information and ideas of the author to what you already know.

W r i t i n g   F o c u s

1. Discuss the meaning of several phrases from a memoir.
2. Sketch a scene that an author describes.
3. Complete a chart that traces and interprets the narrator's conflicting feelings.
4. Write an interpretive paragraph based on a poem.
5. Express your opinion about a statement in an author's work.

One Seeing the Details

Critical Reading

FOCUS

William Least Heat Moon on perspective:

"I was on a Ferris wheel, moving along, seeing far horizons, coming close to earth, rising again, moving, moving, but all the time turning in the same orbit."

BACKGROUND

Blue Highways: A Journey Into America is a reflective memoir chronicling the circular route William Least Heat Moon traveled around America on its back roads. Along the way he discovered his Native American roots. Having just lost his job and wife, Least Heat Moon set out with a "numbing sense that life inevitably creeps toward the absurd." He hoped that the journey would provide "a tonic of curiosity" and help him to see life with fresh vision.

➤ In the excerpt, Least Heat Moon quotes Walt Whitman (1819–1892), a poet who himself spent a great deal of time walking around and observing New York City. By citing Whitman's "profound lesson of reception," Least Heat Moon urges himself to pay attention to new things, other things than have up to this point in his life engaged him. Reviews of *Blue Highways* praised his power of observation: "Least Heat Moon seeks and finds a small-town America where people worry less about making a living than about making a life."

FOR DISCUSSION AND REFLECTION

➤ Why do people travel? What is the lure of an open road? (Responses will vary.)

➤ Ask students to think about a time when an unfamiliar place caused them to see themselves and the world in a new way. (Responses will vary.)

➤ Heat Moon, William's father, told him that "a traveler who misses the journey misses about all he's going to get." Invite students to restate this paternal advice in their own words.

➤ What is the lesson that Least Heat Moon takes away from his father's advice? (That he should pay close attention to the things that happen along the path of his life rather than focus solely on his destination.)

Writing

QUICK ASSESS

Do students' notes:

✓ offer thoughtful interpretations?

✓ pay attention to the details?

Students are asked to interpret phrases from the excerpt. Remind them that forming questions is an important step towards understanding a piece of literature and encourage them to include several possible interpretations of each phrase.

READING AND WRITING EXTENSIONS

➤ Another famous highway memoir is Jack Kerouac's *On the Road*. This classic from the Beat Generation has a tone very different from William Least Heat Moon's memoir. Read a passage to students that captures the peripatetic pacing of these travels and have them share their reactions.

➤ Have students pay very close attention to the trip they take today from school to home. When they arrive home they should write down every detail they remember of what they saw and how they felt on this journey. Invite them to think about how paying attention to details affected the journey itself.

Two Seeing the Literal Meaning

Critical Reading

FOCUS
Rachel Carson on the natural world:

"The beauty of the living world I was trying to save has always been uppermost in my mind—that, and anger at the senseless, brutish things that were being done."

BACKGROUND
Rachel Carson was a marine biologist at the U.S. Bureau of Fisheries. She wrote books about the natural world she observed and deeply loved. Carson's writing explores humans' interactions with the natural world. Her books on the sea, *Under the Sea Wind* and *The Sea Around Us*, were serialized in *The New Yorker*, but she is best known for *The Silent Spring*, which details the dangers of pesticides to the environment. Many identify the publication of this book in 1962 as the birth of the environmental movement. In it Carson asks, "What has silenced the voices of spring in countless towns in America?" Her answer brought an angry response from the chemical industry which accused her of being hysterical and an extremist. But the documentation for her argument was impressive and withstood the test of time. In 1970 the Environmental Protection Agency was established in large part because of the concerns and the consciousness that Rachel Carson raised.

➤ In this excerpt from *The Edge of the Sea*, Carson describes in great detail and specificity the ecology of a tidepool. She brings a deep knowledge of science to her observations and reports what she sees in a language that reflects the wonder she feels.

FOR DISCUSSION AND REFLECTION
➤ What do Carson's references to the magical nature of the physical world suggest about how she views tidepool flora and fauna? (Answers may vary but could include the idea that there is much to wonder at, much we do not yet understand.)

➤ Is this the kind of description you would expect from a scientist? (Carson sees with both the eyes of a poet and the eyes of a biologist. She is a keen observer of the literal world yet at the same time a poetic interpreter of what she sees.)

➤ How does this passage demonstrate her respect for the natural world? (She enters the tidepool only with its permission: "such swells were long enough to admit me." The smallest creature is connected to man, "that intricate fabric of life by which one creature is linked with another, and each with its surroundings.")

Writing

QUICK ASSESS
Do students' sketches:

✓ reflect careful reading?

✓ translate Carson's words into visual images?

✓ focus on Carson's descriptive details?

Students are asked to sketch what they saw in their mind's eye while reading Carson's description. Assure them that it is their ability to visualize and not their ability to draw that is important here.

READING AND WRITING EXTENSIONS
➤ During the 1992 presidential campaign Al Gore was labeled "Ozone Man" because of his support for environmental causes. Have students write a letter to him expressing their views about wildlife preservation.

➤ Have students select a chapter from his book *The Earth in the Balance* and report on the aspect of environmental danger Gore describes.

Three Observing and Interpreting

Critical Reading

FOCUS

Edward Abbey, as a writer, knows the importance of observation:

"May your trails be crooked, winding, lonesome, dangerous, and leading to the most amazing view."

BACKGROUND

In 1948 at age twenty-one Edward Abbey left the family farm in Pennsylvania and set off to see the American West. He fell in love with the desert, a love that shaped his life and art for more than forty years. Abbey wrote extensively about the West and the dangers posed by overdevelopment. He was an eloquent advocate for the preservation of wilderness.

➤ In this excerpt from "Freedom and Wilderness" Abbey tells the story of the day he saw a mountain lion. While his style is laced with irony ("I was caretaker and head janitor of a 70,000 acre wildlife refuge"), the narrator's stance toward the animal is one of wonder ("I haven't seen a mountain lion since that evening, but the experience remains shining in my memory"). The encounter both terrifies him and engenders a "kind of affection and the crazy desire to communicate, to make some kind of emotional, even physical contact with the animal."

FOR DISCUSSION AND REFLECTION

➤ Ask students how they interpreted the fact that the mountain lion seemed to be following the narrator? (Reasonable interpretations include that the lion wants to communicate with the man, curiosity on the part of the animal, and malice—though Abbey knows that mountain lions rarely attack humans.)

➤ What in the story demonstrates Abbey's respect for wildlife? (Abbey expresses the hope that his children's children will discover how to get close enough to the animal to shake paws with it—a sign of mutual respect—and to learn from it.)

Writing

QUICK ASSESS

Do students' charts:

✓ interpret what the details mean to the author?

✓ include a range of Abbey's observations?

Students are asked to chart the narrator's conflicting feelings over the course of the story and then attempt to interpret them. As they speculate on what they believe Abbey wants the reader to understand, remind them that there is no single "right" answer, but answers must be consistent with what they have inferred about Abbey's attitudes. As Kent Duryee wrote of Abbey, "Placing a label on Edward Abbey would be akin to picking up all the grains of sand in the desert Southwest, putting them in a large glass container, and labeling that container 'Desert.' What Abbey wrote about was the Earth, and his deep love of it."

READING AND WRITING EXTENSIONS

➤ Read students the following quote and ask them to interpret Abbey's instructions: "Do not jump into your automobile next June and rush out to the Canyon country hoping to see some of that which I have attempted to evoke in these pages. In the first place you can't see anything from a car; you've got to get out of the contraption and walk, better yet crawl, on hands and knees, over the sandstone and through the cactus. When traces of blood begin to mark your trail you'll see something, maybe."

➤ Have students write about a time when the behavior of an animal (a zoo animal, a family pet) puzzled them.

Four Looking Beneath the Surface

Critical Reading

FOCUS

Active readers look beneath the surface to discover the ideas below.

BACKGROUND

This lesson asks students to see how a poet can take a simple, familiar object — the mushroom, for example — and manipulate it to convey an observation about life or human nature. One place to begin is by brainstorming with students everything they know about mushrooms: their size, flavor, texture, uses, habitat, growth patterns. If students are relatively unfamiliar with them, turn to the encyclopedia.

➤ In her poem "Mushrooms," Sylvia Plath (1932–1963) ostensibly describes the characteristics of mushrooms. Beneath the surface of this literal account, Plath is describing a particular kind of person. The job of the reader is to figure out exactly what kind of person she means. Notice Plath's word choice for describing mushroom behavior: "Whitely, discreetly, / Very quietly," "Diet on water, / On crumbs of shadow, / Bland-mannered, asking / Little or nothing." Insuring that the reader does not mistake this poem for a botany lesson, Plath uses human body parts to describe the mushroom's features: "our toes, our noses," "Soft fists," "Earless and eyeless, / Perfectly voiceless."

FOR DISCUSSION AND REFLECTION

➤ Ask students why they think Plath personifes the mushrooms. (She compares mushrooms to some people. Though quiet and small, they are powerful and will "by morning / Inherit the earth.")

➤ Ask students what qualities they ordinarily associate with mushrooms. (Answers will vary.)

Writing

QUICK ASSESS

Do students' paragraphs:

✓ recognize both the literal and interpretive levels of the poem?

✓ demonstrate an understanding of the poem?

✓ refer to specific attributes Plath has given to the mushrooms?

Students are asked to use their understanding of the poem to write an interpretive paragraph, explaining how a type of person or object is like the mushrooms Plath describes. Have them refer to their list of qualities and attributes as they begin.

READING AND WRITING EXTENSIONS

➤ *The Bell Jar*, Sylvia Plath's only novel, describes the mental breakdown, attempted suicide, and eventual recovery of a young college girl. The circumstances of the fictional Esther Greenwood's life are very similar to Plath's. Plath, in fact, wrote the book from her bed in a psychiatric ward. Teenagers respond very powerfully to the story. Have interested students read the book and report back to the class about what they have read.

➤ Have students choose another ordinary fruit or vegetable and write a poem of their own in which they use it to describe human characteristics.

Five Comprehending Critically

C r i t i c a l   R e a d i n g

FOCUS

Critical comprehension involves "reading behind the lines."

BACKGROUND

If literal comprehension is seen as "reading the lines" and interpretive comprehension is "reading between the lines," critical comprehension can be described as "reading behind the lines." When readers ask questions about the significance and relevance of the material, they are going beyond the words on the page. Questions to signal critical comprehension include "So what?" or "How is this related to anything else I know?" or "How can I use this information or these ideas?"

➤ This lesson invites students to explore one aspect of critical comprehension— using information from the passage to express their own opinions. Students need to concentrate on understanding Least Heat Moon's point and constructing their own response.

FOR DISCUSSION AND REFLECTION

➤ In the excerpt from *Blue Highways*, William Least Heat Moon describes himself as a witness. What does he mean? (Although a common understanding of "witness" is within a courtroom context, Least Heat Moon means something broader. He uses the word in the sense of someone who has been called upon to be present at a transaction to testify that it has taken place. The transaction that Least Heat Moon witnesses is that between the American people and the land that makes up their country: "In my own country, I had gone out, had met, had shared. I had stood as witness.")

➤ Ask students to put into their own words Black Elk's explanation of the significance of circles in the world. Are Black Elk's and Least Heat Moon's ways of explaining changes congruent with or at odds with students' views? (Responses will vary.)

W r i t i n g

QUICK ASSESS

Do students' responses:

✓ clearly state their opinion?

✓ include reasons and examples for their opinions?

Students are asked to express their opinion about one statement in the excerpt. Using critical comprehension requires them to support their opinion with reasons and examples from the text and their own experience.

READING AND WRITING EXTENSIONS

➤ Ask students to use Least Heat Moon's reflections as a model for their own. They should select an experience in which they learned something and summarize their learning as Least Heat Moon has.

➤ Have students underline particularly expressive phrases from this excerpt and then rearrange them into a found poem.

PERSPECTIVES ON A SUBJECT: THE VIETNAM WAR

Unit Overview

In this unit, students will explore the different perspectives from which a subject can be approached. By reading an objective historical account, a subjective memoir, and a poem about the Vietnam War, students will learn to distinguish among different points of view, differentiate between fact and opinion, and appreciate the value of examining a subject from multiple perspectives.

Literature Focus

	Lesson	Literature
1.	Presenting a Subject	**Barry Denenberg,** from *Voices from Vietnam* (Nonfiction)
2.	Using Supporting Material	**Barry Denenberg,** from *Voices from Vietnam* (Nonfiction)
3.	Firsthand Experience	**Le Ly Hayslip,** from *When Heaven and Earth Changed Places* (Nonfiction)
4.	Different Genres	**W. D. Ehrhart,** "The Next Step" (Poetry)
5.	Comparing Perspectives	

Reading Focus

1. A critical reader examines all of the evidence, carefully considering what are facts and what are opinions, before deciding what to believe.
2. When a writer wants to present an objective account, he or she must provide as many different views of the event or idea as possible.
3. Accounts of firsthand experience can provide insights into a topic that objective accounts cannot.
4. A poem can provide a valuable perspective on a subject because its dense, reflective language can make a concise, yet potent, emotional statement.
5. To understand a subject fully, it is important to examine it from many perspectives.

Writing Focus

1. Identify and evaluate facts and opinions in a passage of nonfiction.
2. Make a generalization about the author's use of evidence, using facts, examples, and quotations as support.
3. Answer questions about two accounts of the Vietnam War—one objective and one subjective.
4. Discuss a poem in several paragraphs, commenting on the value of a poetic perspective.
5. Rewrite one of the selections, using a different point of view or genre.

One Presenting a Subject

Critical Reading

FOCUS

Active readers evaluate evidence by asking questions about its source. They know how to discriminate between fact and opinion.

BACKGROUND

This excerpt is taken from the first two chapters of Barry Denenberg's *Voices from Vietnam*. The complete work includes quotations from hundreds of individuals involved in the Vietnam War on all sides of the conflict—from nurses to presidents, from soldiers to civilians. Denenberg provides a narrative backbone for the voices which make up his story.

➤ In these first pages Denenberg outlines the historical events that led up to American involvement in Vietnam. He explains what happened without ostensible commentary: "The North would be ruled by Ho Chi Minh's communists and the South by the recently formed government of Ngo Dinh Diem. President Eisenhower backed the anti-Communist Diem and praised him as a 'miracle man.' The United States supported him with money and material."

FOR DISCUSSION AND REFLECTION

➤ What does the fact that the French called their war in Vietnam "the dirty war" suggest to you about their attitudes towards the people, the country, the military struggle? (It shows little respect for the culture or the suffering of the Vietnamese people. The whole entanglement was a messy, unpleasant affair that brought honor to no one.)

➤ Is the domino theory a theory or a fact? (As the word "theory" suggests, the domino theory is one view about how countries behave, not an observable scientific phenomenon.)

➤ How does the closing quote from Chester Cooper of the Central Intelligence Agency affect your opinion about the reliability of the evidence as presented? (Someone from the C.I.A. is likely to know what its mission was in Vietnam and is therefore likely to be a reliable source.)

Writing

QUICK ASSESS

Do students' evaluations:

✓ identify the differences between fact and opinion?

✓ recognize supporting evidence?

✓ judge the reliability of a source?

Students are asked to evaluate the historical accuracy of the excerpt. Remind them that the basis for their judgment need not be prior knowledge of the Vietnam War. What they must do is assess the reliability of Denenberg's information.

READING AND WRITING EXTENSIONS

➤ Barry Denenberg's *Voices from Vietnam* was named an ALA Best Book for Young Adults. Students interested in learning more about this period of history would find it both engaging and informative. Have students find other books on the Vietnam War and share them in two-minute oral reports with the class.

➤ Have students become oral historians and interview adults they know about their perspectives on American involvement in Vietnam.

TWO Using Supporting Material

Critical Reading

FOCUS
An "objective" account is one that has not been influenced by personal feelings or opinions.

BACKGROUND
One measure of the objectivity of Barry Denenberg's text is the extent to which he provides information from many different sources. On the controversial subject of Ngo Dinh Diem and his government, for example, the author offers evidence and quotations from Jan Barry of the U.S. Army and from Truong Nhu Tang, a Vietcong. Later in this chapter, when the problem Truong Nhu Tang has described between the Christian Diem and the Buddhists escalates and Buddhist monks set themselves on fire in protest, Denenberg lets Madam Nhu speak for herself: "Let them burn and we shall clap our hands."

➤ Here you have three different sources cited on the subject of Diem and Diem's methods of government. You know the speakers have not collaborated on their statements. A conclusion drawn on the basis of such evidence is likely to be accurate.

FOR DISCUSSION AND REFLECTION
➤ How would you characterize Denenberg's writing style? (Responses will vary but should focus on the unemotional, simple, straightforward reporting.)

➤ Why do you think he chooses to write in this manner? (The drama is in the unfolding of the story his facts will tell. He does not want to interfere with the reader's reception of this information by using emotional language of his own.)

Writing

QUICK ASSESS
Do students' writings:

✔ offer a generalization about the author's use of evidence?

✔ cite facts, examples, and quotations as support?

Students may have difficulty making a generalization about Denenberg's use of evidence. If necessary, offer sentence stems such as "Denenberg's evidence is not objective because…" or "Although Denenberg's prose is objective, the quotations are subjective opinions because…."

READING AND WRITING EXTENSIONS
➤ Ask students to make a list of other people whose views about Ngo Dinh Diem would add to their picture of the man. (For example, his servant, President Eisenhower, a South Vietnamese soldier, a Buddhist monk. No need for names.)

➤ Have students think about a time when an event they witnessed (a car accident, a fight in class, a football game) was described by someone else who was also there but somehow saw things very differently. Ask them to write about how they felt when this happened.

Three Firsthand Experience

Critical Reading

FOCUS

From Merriam Webster's *Encyclopedia of Literature:*

"A memoir is a narrative composed from personal experience and acquaintance with the events, scenes, or persons described."

BACKGROUND

A memoir differs from an autobiography chiefly in the degree of emphasis placed on external events. Where writers of autobiography are concerned primarily with their whole lives as subject matter, writers of memoir usually focus on fewer events, and their main purpose is to describe or interpret those events.

➤ Le Ly Hayslip's memoir, *When Heaven and Earth Changed Places*, is described by the author as "a Vietnamese woman's journey from war to peace." In this excerpt she returns to Vietnam in order to find her father. What she finds both in the person of her father and in the state of her village shocks and saddens her deeply.

FOR DISCUSSION AND REFLECTION

➤ Ask students to identify lines and phrases that struck them as they read. Have them try to explain why they think Hayslip's words had this effect. (In many cases it will be an appeal to their senses: sensory details of sight, sound, taste, touch, smell.)

➤ How did the father's detailed analysis of American involvement in Vietnam reveal that Hayslip was writing about events years after they occured? (When she arrives, the father is almost dead, coughing up blood and barely able to speak. Within moments of her arrival, Hayslip relates a remarkably cogent philosophical commentary that he offered her as she sobbed in his arms. It is likely that Hayslip has combined several conversations into one.)

Writing

QUICK ASSESS

Do students' answers:

✔ reflect an understanding of the differences between objective and subjective reporting?

✔ state which account they prefer?

✔ demonstrate an awareness of the effect each account can have on a reader?

The first writing task asks students to detail what they have learned from this passage about the effects of the Vietnam War on the Vietnamese people. The second asks students to note the differences between an objective account like Denenberg's and a subjective account like Le Ly Hayslip's. Finally, as they explain which they prefer, be sure that students are clear about the strengths and weakness of both types of reporting.

READING AND WRITING EXTENSIONS

➤ Tim O'Brien, author of *If I Die in a Combat Zone Box Me Up and Ship Me Home* and *The Things They Carried*, wrote:

"It still boils down to suffering, and the thing about Vietnam that most bothers me is that it is treated as a political experience, a sociological experience, and the human element of what a soldier goes through—and what the Vietnamese went through—is not only neglected: it is almost cast aside as superfluous."

Ask students to summarize O'Brien's point in their own words.

➤ Have students search for another memoir about a war experience. Invite them to share passages from it with the class.

Four Different Genres

Critical Reading

FOCUS

Aristotle on the nature of poetry:

"Poetry is a more philosophic and a finer thing than history, since poetry speaks of universals and history only of particulars."

BACKGROUND

Ask students to compare the quote from Aristotle with W. D. Ehrhart's observation that "Scholars and politicians, journalists and generals may argue, write and re-write 'the facts.' But when a poem is written, it becomes a singular entity with an inextinguishable and unalterable life of its own. It is a true reflection of the feelings and perceptions it records, and as such, it is as valuable a document as any history ever written."

➤ Invite students to think about other historical/poetic juxtapositions—Shakespeare's *Julius Caesar*, for example, with a passage from a history book about ancient Rome.

➤ "The Next Step" expresses the fear foot soldiers experience with every step as they march through enemy territory. The poem details the specific dangers (ambushes, tripwires, mines, sniper's bullets) in a repetitive pattern that suggests whatever the danger, the fear is the same. The seventh stanza does not say what "may" happen; it invites the reader to fill in the open space on the page with other, unnamed dangers. The final three lines omit the words "you take," implying that the walking soldier may have fallen and may never take "the next step." Or, they could imply that the march continues beyond the soldier's willingness to think about the danger.

FOR DISCUSSION AND REFLECTION

➤ How does the use of the second person pronoun "you" in the poem affect you as a reader? (It draws you into the poem. This isn't happening to somebody else. It is happening to you.)

➤ Is this poem specifically about the Vietnam War the way Barry Denenberg's text and Le Ly Hayslip's memoir were? (Ehrhart's poem has a more universal theme. The particulars could be applied to any modern war.)

Writing

QUICK ASSESS

Do students' paragraphs:

✔ discuss details of the poem and speculate on the author's strategies?

✔ examine how a poem can provide a valuable perspective on a subject?

As students begin to analyze Ehrhart's poem, have them think about how he uses repetition, rhythm, and dramatic details to express emotions and feelings.

READING AND WRITING EXTENSIONS

➤ In *Shrapnel in the Heart: Letters and Remembrances from the Vietnam Veterans Memorial*, Laura Palmer has collected notes, poems, and photographs that visitors have left at the wall of the Vietnam Veterans Memorial in Washington, D. C. Share some of these with students and ask them to reflect upon how these "particular" remembrances have "universal" significance.

➤ Discuss with students how we use repetition and dramatic details in our regular speech. Then have students create a poem out of ordinary talk.

Five Comparing Perspectives

Critical Reading

FOCUS

Reading about the Vietnam War from different perspectives creates a more complete picture of what happened than any one view could ever provide.

BACKGROUND

Students have read three very different texts about the Vietnam War: Barry Denenberg's historical account, Le Ly Hayslip's memoir, and W. D. Ehrhart's poem. Often students' only exposure to history occurs through textbook summaries of events. This collection of readings will help them begin to understand how much the retelling of a story is influenced by a writer's point of view.

FOR DISCUSSION AND REFLECTION

➤ If you were to rate these three writers for objectivity, who would score highest? (Denenberg attempts to present a balanced view while Hayslip and Ehrhart only intend to express their own purposely limited points of view. This makes Denenberg's account the most objective.)

➤ If you were to rate these three writers for their success in making you as a reader care about their subject, who would score highest? (This is a matter of personal inclination. Ask students to support their opinion with quotations from the selection.)

Writing

QUICK ASSESS

Do students' writings:

✔ recast the original piece from another perspective?

✔ use details from the original?

Help students develop possible ideas for rewriting one of these passages from another perspective. Further suggestions include a poem using words and phrases from Denenberg's essay, a diary entry by the commanding officer who sent the soldier in Ehrhart's poem out to the field, an interview between Barry Denenberg and Le Ly Hayslip, or a review of Hayslip's memoir by an American Vietnam War veteran.

READING AND WRITING EXTENSIONS

➤ Eve Bunting's picture book for children called *The Wall* tells the story of a small boy and his father who visit the Vietnam Veterans Memorial in Washington to find the name of the boy's grandfather. The story is told from the point of view of the young child. Read the book to students and discuss how this particular perspective on the Vietnam War is striking for the way it explores the lasting impact of this war and all wars. Although the child is proud of his grandfather, he tells his father that "I'd rather have my grandpa here, taking me to the river, telling me to button my jacket because it's cold. I'd rather have him here."

➤ Have students write a letter from Le Ly Hayslip to W. D. Ehrhart. What might she want to say to him?

Unit Overview

In "Shades of Meaning," students will explore the rich colors available with language. By examining tone, mood, figurative language, and connotative meanings, students will learn how paying attention to words and their shades of meaning helps them understand what a writer is trying to say. Students will practice their close reading skills on a variety of poems and a nonfiction excerpt.

Literature Focus

	Lesson	Literature
1.	Close Reading	**Shel Silverstein,** "Colors" (Poetry) **Naomi Shihab Nye,** "Defining White" (Poetry)
2.	Comparing to Define	
3.	Scientific and Poetic Language	**Diane Ackerman,** from *A Natural History of the Senses* (Nonfiction)
4.	Establishing Mood	**Juan Ramón Jiménez,** "Landscape in Scarlet" from *Platero and I* (Poetry)
5.	Visualizing Words	**Joy Harjo,** "Visions" (Poetry)

Reading Focus

1. Selecting lines from a poem and writing your own ideas in response is a kind of close reading. This technique makes you a partner with the poet.
2. Defining words through similes and metaphors is one way to clarify the shades of meaning in your language.
3. Some people tend to think of scientific writing as dry and objective. But it can also be personal and poetic, without losing its factual nature.
4. Good readers often focus on the mood of a piece of literature because it helps them understand their reaction to it.
5. Writers help us see the pictures in their writing either by using direct description or by using symbols that allow us to visualize the specifics.

Writing Focus

1. Write a short essay about the meaning of words.
2. Write a poem that uses similes and metaphors to define a color.
3. Analyze the scientific and poetic language in a passage of nonfiction.
4. Create a sketch depicting the mood of a poetic passage.
5. Describe how you visualize a poem.

One Close Reading

Critical Reading

FOCUS

A close reading of a text requires that we pay careful attention to the pictures writers paint with words.

BACKGROUND

Color exists in our minds. What we see and call "color" is actually light reflected from the objects around us. When a flower looks red to us, it is reflecting red light into our eyes. Writers use words to create in a reader's mind's eye the colors that they see in theirs. The challenge for both reader and writer is that words can be slippery things and colors particularly difficult to pin down.

➤ In Naomi Shihab Nye's poem "Defining White," the narrator struggles with the problem of explaining the shade of white she wants, presumably for paint, to someone over the phone. Insisting that she wants "white-white, / that tends in no direction / other than itself," she begins to muse on how her demand is not as simple as she first thought: "Now this is getting complex. / Every white I see is tending / toward something else."

FOR DISCUSSION AND REFLECTION

➤ Why does the speaker say that her husband knows what white is? (As a photographer, he has a great deal of experience with the two absolutes of black and white "and all the gray neighborhoods in between.")

➤ What does Shihab Nye suggest in her closing question, "Is wind a noun or a verb?" (The same four letters denote both the verb wind, as in to wind a clock, and the noun wind, as in moving air. The difficulty the poet has had "defining white" is not a problem limited to color but extends to much of language.)

Writing

QUICK ASSESS

Do students' essays:

✓ explain how various shades of meaning can be ascribed to a single word?

✓ discuss how poets use these shades of meaning to explore complex ideas?

Students are asked to explain how they have observed the meanings of words sliding into other shades of meaning. It may help to introduce this writing assignment by drawing students' attention to words with seemingly straightforward definitions that can mean quite different things to different people. For example, "keys" to a homeowner suggest security, while to a prisoner they mean freedom. To a teenager with his first car, "keys" equal independence.

READING AND WRITING EXTENSIONS

➤ Bring to class a box of 64 Crayola crayons. Have students choose one color crayon and, using the name of this color in their title, write a poem called "Defining…"—for example, "Defining Midnight Blue" or "Defining Magenta." They should feel free to range widely when defining their color, as Naomi Shihab Nye has in her poem.

➤ Octavio Paz uses many different colors in his short story "The Blue Bouquet." Read the story to students. First have students identify all the color words in the story and then discuss their significance.

Two Comparing to Define

Critical Reading

FOCUS

Naomi Shihab Nye on poetic perception:

"Writing helped me notice more, kept me tuned up like an instrument."

BACKGROUND

Naomi Shihab Nye's poem "Defining White" is a study in the difficulty of pinning down a color with words. Often when a term eludes simple definition we resort to comparison, often using figurative language. We call such figures of speech similes and metaphors. In a simile, the resemblance between two unlike entities is explicitly indicated by the words "like" or "as." (My grandmother's hair is white as snow.) In a metaphor, a word or phrase denoting one kind of object or action is used in place of another to suggest a likeness or analogy between them. (Her midnight eyes met mine.) Remind students that a metaphor is an implied comparison.

FOR DISCUSSION AND REFLECTION

➤ In his book *An Anthropologist on Mars*, neurologist and writer Oliver Sacks tells the story of a painter who as a result of a car accident becomes totally colorblind. Discuss why colorblindness would be particularly painful for an artist. Sacks writes that, "His despair of conveying what his world looked like, and the uselessness of the usual black-and-white analogies, finally drove the artist to create an entire grey room, a grey universe, in his studio, in which tables, chairs, and an elaborate dinner ready for serving were all painted in a range of greys" (p. 10). How would this solution bring the artist relief? (Responses will vary.)

➤ How do similes and metaphors differ in the effects they have on readers? (Responses will vary, but encourage students to cite specific examples.)

Writing

QUICK ASSESS

Do students' poems:

✓ make use of similes and metaphors to define a color?

✓ demonstrate a range of strategies for describing an abstract idea?

Offer students the option of beginning their poems as Naomi Shihab Nye has done—with a reason to define the color in great specificity. Discuss possible scenarios when someone might need to identify a color with precision.

READING AND WRITING EXTENSIONS

➤ Synesthesia is the evocation or transposition of one sense by another. It is a device much used in poetry. For example, Edith Sitwell refers to "the enormous and gold-rayed rustling sun." The line is striking because we do not usually think of the sun making noise. Invite students to write about a color using synesthesia—that is, without employing the sense of sight (for example, the sound of blue, the smell of red, or the taste of purple).

➤ In the story "The Country of the Blind" by H. G. Wells, fourteen generations of people have been blind and cut off from the seeing world. Over the years the names for all the things of sight had faded and changed: "Much of their imagination had shriveled with their eyes, and they had made for themselves new imaginations with their ever more sensitive ears and fingertips." Ask students to imagine what else might be different in this country of the blind.

Three Scientific and Poetic Language

Critical Reading

FOCUS

From *A Natural History of the Senses*:

"Sunlight rules most living things with its golden edicts. When the days begin to shorten, soon after the summer solstice on June 21, a tree reconsiders its leaves."

Scientific writing can be personal and poetic.

BACKGROUND

Poets and scientists use language in very different ways. While the scientist is always searching to find the most precise words to denote objects and processes with great specificity, the poet often revels in the various connotations of a word. In scientific notation, H_2O refers to the substance water which is made up of two parts hydrogen and one part oxygen. In a poem, *water* may suggest cleansing, refreshment, or the state of being wet.

➤ While the multiple connotations of a word are anathema to the scientist, they can be a joy to the poet. Denotation is the explicit meaning of a word. Connotation is the implied meaning of a word including its primary meaning.

➤ When Diane Ackerman describes why leaves turn color in the fall, she writes with the detail of a scientist and the sensibility of a poet.

FOR DISCUSSION AND REFLECTION

➤ Ask students to explain what they think Diane Ackerman means when she writes, "a tree reconsiders its leaves." What is striking about the way the writer has phrased this idea? (In the fall the role of a leaf in the life of a tree changes. "Reconsiders" is a verb usually ascribed to human behavior. Her use of this word in a novel context causes the sensitive reader to look with fresh eyes at the tree.)

➤ Can Ackerman's writing be called a hybrid? (Literally, a hybrid is a plant or animal that is the offspring of two different species or varieties. It is also defined as something made by combining two different elements. Responses will vary.)

Writing

QUICK ASSESS

Do students' answers:

✓ identify passages from the excerpt as "scientific" or "poetic"?

✓ explain their classification of Ackerman's writing?

As students analyze Ackerman's language and attempt to classify her writing, remind them to cite lines from the excerpt as evidence for their generalizations. You might also point out that it is possibly the fact that Ackerman's writing is hard to classify that has made it popular.

READING AND WRITING EXTENSIONS

➤ In her book *A Natural History of the Senses*, Diane Ackerman explores each of the senses using a compilation of scientific data and poetic reflections. Students will particularly enjoy her short essays on "The Psychopharmacology of Chocolate" and "Sneezing." You might want to follow this last essay with the A. A. Milne poem "Sneezles" and have students write about their reactions to each.

➤ Have students go to the library to research the five senses and then compile a class list of surprising facts about them.

Four Establishing Mood

Critical Reading

FOCUS

Mood is the feeling or tone conveyed by a literary or artistic work.

BACKGROUND

This chapter from *Platero and I* describes how, for a brief period of time, a sunset can magically transform the landscape and all who inhabit it. Juan Ramón Jiménez begins with the evocative title "Landscape in Scarlet" and proceeds to detail the effect the setting sun has on everything within its reach. The sun itself is "bleeding purple and crimson" causing green pine trees to turn "vaguely red." Under the spell of the sun, the narrator's donkey, Platero, has his "black eyes turned to scarlet" and drinks of the "crimson, violet, rose-colored" water.

➤ The speaker feels "entranced," and though he knows this place well in ordinary light, the sunset has so altered it that "at any moment an unearthly adventure may befall us" or "an abandoned castle" appear.

FOR DISCUSSION AND REFLECTION

➤ Reread the passage from *Platero and I* aloud and ask students to describe the feeling or tone that Jiménez's language conveyed to them. Can they think of times in their life when they have felt this way, places or moments that have inspired this kind of awe?

➤ Make a list of words on the board that characterize this mood. (Possible responses are *calm, quiet, reflective, pensive, peaceful, eerie, charged.*)

➤ What are the denotations and connotations of Platero's name? (denotations: silver, a precious metal; connotations: a valuable companion, a rare friend)

➤ What is the significance of the final line, "Come, Platero"? (That though the feeling created by the sunset is one of infinity, the sunset itself is finite. It is time for them to move on.)

Writing

QUICK ASSESS

Do students' sketches:

✓ reflect a sensitivity to the mood of Jiménez's writing?

✓ use particular images from the passage?

✓ have a descriptive title?

Before students begin their sketches, have them share their charts about how mood is created. Discuss how the mood would change if the author had substituted different colors, used fewer adjectives, or avoided figurative language.

READING AND WRITING EXTENSIONS

➤ Painters and musicians also use colors to create a mood. Have students write freely as you play for them blues or jazz music such as John Coltrane's "Blue Train" or Robert Johnson's solos. See if their writing reflects the melancholy and complaint characteristic of this style of melody.

➤ Show students reproductions of paintings such as Edward Hopper's *Night Hawks* or Georges Seurat's *A Sunday Afternoon on the Island of La Grand Jatte* and have them write about how the colors these artists chose created a distinctive mood.

Five Visualizing Words

Critical Reading

FOCUS

Active readers visualize the words on a page in living color.

BACKGROUND

Like the Greek goddess Iris, poets travel the path of the rainbow to bring messages to people on earth. Unlike the goddess, they travel metaphorically. In the physical world, a rainbow results when raindrops in the air bend and reflect the rays of the sun. It could be argued that in a metaphorical world a poem results when crafted words bend and reflect light from within.

➤ In "Visions," Joy Harjo uses the image of a rainbow to bring people the news of the "color / horses that were within us all of this time." A rainbow touches down near her friend's mother's house in Isleta. She, the poet, has the vision to see in this rainbow "Bright horses" rolling "over / and over the dusking sky." She has "heard the thunder of their beating / hearts" and writes this poem to tell us what she has seen and heard. Prophetically she informs us that "All the colors of horses formed the rainbow, / and formed us / watching them."

➤ Joy Harjo is a professor of English at the University of Arizona, an editor, a screenwriter, and a player of tenor sax. A member of the Creek tribe, she was born in Tulsa, Oklahoma. Along with writing poetry, Joy Harjo performs with a jazz band, Poetic Justice.

FOR DISCUSSION AND REFLECTION

➤ What are the denotations and connotations of the title of the town Isleta? (denotation: little island; connotation: an isolated, desolate spot where they didn't see horses because there "we wait for the easiest vision / to save us")

➤ What is the significance of the appearance of the rainbow in Isleta? (Harjo describes the occurrence as "a crack / in the universe.")

➤ The "dusking sky" refers to what time of day? (Sunset, as Juan Ramón Jiménez describes in lesson four, is a magical time.)

Writing

QUICK ASSESS

Do students' descriptions:

✓ identify important visual words?

✓ explain how they visualized the rainbow?

Before they begin to write, remind students that Harjo is using the rainbow of horses as a metaphor. Help them to speculate on possible interpretations. Help them see the rainbow of horses as a metaphor for the unrecognized richness, color, beauty, and power within all of us.

READING AND WRITING EXTENSIONS

➤ In her collection *She Had Some Horses*, Harjo's title poem makes powerful use of repetition: "She had horses who laughed too much. / She had horses who threw rocks at glass houses. / She had horses who licked razor blades." Read the entire poem aloud and ask students to describe the effect such repetition has upon a reader.

➤ Using Harjo's poem as a model, have students write a poem beginning with a rainbow.

WORDS IN CONTEXT

Unit Overview

The selections in "Words in Context"—all about food—invite students to focus on an author's vocabulary. As they read and respond to the writing of James Agee, M.F. K. Fisher, and Margaret Atwood, students will explore how by using present tense, familiar words in unfamiliar ways, and good sensory details, writers can create powerful effects. In addition, students will think about how the words writers use to describe a culture can illuminate its distinctiveness.

Literature Focus

	Lesson	Literature
1.	Sensory Language	**James Agee,** from *Let Us Now Praise Famous Men* (Nonfiction)
2.	Familiar Words in Unfamiliar Ways	
3.	Words and Social History	**M. F. K. Fisher,** from *Serve It Forth* (Nonfiction)
4.	Simple Words, Complex Ideas	**Margaret Atwood,** "Bread" (Nonfiction)
5.	The Power of the Present Tense	

Reading Focus

1. Being aware of how a writer uses sensory details enables you to understand a scene more fully.

2. Writers sometimes use familiar words in unfamiliar ways to call attention to the sensory and emotional details of a scene.

3. Focusing on the language writers use to describe a culture enables you to understand its distinctiveness.

4. Simple, everyday words, when used carefully, may create powerful images and strong emotions.

5. Writers create powerful effects when they use such strategies as addressing the reader and writing in the present tense.

Writing Focus

1. Write a descriptive paragraph, using sensory details.

2. Write a description that uses familiar words in unfamiliar ways.

3. Describe a culture's food habits.

4. Interpret and respond to a passage of nonfiction.

5. Write an essay about a familiar, concrete object.

One Sensory Language

Critical Reading

FOCUS

By appealing to our senses, James Agee allows us to see, hear, smell, touch, and taste the food he describes:

"The biscuits are large and shapeless, not cut round, and are pale, not tanned, and are dusty with flour. They taste of flour and soda and damp salt and fill the mouth stickily."

BACKGROUND

In 1936, James Agee and Walker Evans were commissioned to write a magazine article on cotton tenantry in the United States, focusing on the daily life of an average white sharecropper family. The article was never published, but Agee's prose and Evans's photographs became the American classic *Let Us Now Praise Famous Men*. The book is difficult to categorize, as it includes philosophy, narrative, satire, cultural history, and autobiography, as well as the reporting the two young men set out to do.

➤ In this selection from that volume, James Agee describes a meal he shared with a sharecropper family in such detail that the active reader can not only see and smell and taste with him, but can also interpret these sensory impressions as a commentary on the lives of those who eat this food every day of their lives. For example, "Of milk I hardly know how to say; it is skimmed, blue-lighted; to a city palate its warmth and odor are somehow dirty and at the same time vital, a little as if one were drinking blood." Thin and unchilled, the milk lacks the richness usually associated with the nourishing substance. A few lines down, "it seems to be this odor, and a sort of wateriness and discouraged tepidity, which combine to make the food seem unclean, sticky, and sallow with some invisible sort of disease." We eat to renew depleted energy. By describing the food as discouraged, Agee suggests an environment of poverty that exhausts people in deep ways.

FOR DISCUSSION AND REFLECTION

➤ Ask students if they found the food Agee describes appetizing. (They will most likely say no, but push students to identify the particular lines and phrases that make the food seem distasteful.)

➤ Reread the last lines of the selection where Agee associates the sight and smell and feel of the food with a "true taste of home." What do these lines suggest about Agee's early years and his attitude toward that time now? (The food would not ordinarily appeal to his adult palate, but because it is charged with memories of home, he digs in with enthusiasm and "no faking of enjoyment at all.")

Writing

QUICK ASSESS

Do students' paragraphs:

✓ include vocabulary from Agee's passage?

✓ indicate that students have learned new words?

✓ make use of rich sensory detail?

As students borrow Agee's words for use in their own descriptive paragraphs about food, allow them to check with classmates and with you if they are uncertain that their usage of an unfamiliar word makes sense.

READING AND WRITING EXTENSIONS

➤ Have students look at Walker Evans's photographs in *Let Us Now Praise Famous Men* and describe what they see in the pictures, using all, or almost all, of their senses. These are powerful images that will likely evoke a discussion of what it means to live in poverty.

➤ Ask students to describe a meal that they wish they could forget.

Two Familiar Words in Unfamiliar Ways

Critical Reading

FOCUS
By using familiar words in surprising contexts, writers wring new meaning out of language.

BACKGROUND
Sophisticated use of vocabulary does not always involve pulling out a thesaurus or employing big words. Often, accomplished writers take everyday words and use them in ways that startle the reader. James Agee is a master of this technique. For example, he gives inanimate objects human characteristics. In the passage from *Let Us Now Praise Famous Men* in Lesson One, he describes biscuits as "pale, not tanned" and the jam as "loose." Agee talks about a "quiet little fight" taking place on your palate and in the pit of your stomach. This is unusual language for describing tastes, yet the result for the reader is a powerful sensory experience of Agee's meal.

FOR DISCUSSION AND REFLECTION
➢ Have students discuss the unusual uses of common words that they found in Agee's passage. Ask them to explain the effect of this surprising usage of words. (Responses will vary.)

➢ Do unfamiliar uses of familiar words slow you down or cause you to reread? (They should. That is one of the author's intended effects.)

Writing

QUICK ASSESS
Do students' descriptions:
✓ appeal to the five senses?
✓ have an emotional context?
✓ use simple words in surprising ways?

As students consider which meal to describe, urge them to pick one that is in some way charged with importance for them—a meal, that like Marcel Proust's crumb of madeleine, could inspire a seven-volume novel. Assure students, however, that their piece need not be this long. Put several familiar descriptive words—such as "crisp" and "spicy"—on the board and brainstorm possible new contexts for them.

READING AND WRITING EXTENSIONS
➢ Magical realist writers often make use of familiar words in unfamiliar contexts. In chapter three of *Like Water for Chocolate*, Laura Esquivel describes a meal whose entree, Quail in Rose Petal Sauce, acts as an aphrodisiac. Using the simple, straightforward language of a recipe, Esquivel reveals the magical properties and power of exquisitely prepared food: "It was as if a strange alchemical process had dissolved her entire being in the rose petal sauce, in the tender flesh of the quails, in the wine, in every one of the meal's aromas." Read this passage to students and ask them to compare it with Agee's style.

➢ Have students create a menu for an ideal meal, giving each item an original and evocative name.

Three Words and Social History

Critical Reading

FOCUS

The language writers use to describe a culture reflects and reveals their stance toward that culture:

"Ox meat was roasted or boiled, but many kinds of little birds, and even quails and ducks, were salted and eaten raw."

BACKGROUND

In *The Art of Eating*, M. F. K. Fisher writes: "People ask me: Why do you write about food, and eating and drinking? Why don't you write about the struggle for power and security, and about love, the way others do? They ask it accusingly, as if I were somehow gross, unfaithful to the honor of my craft. The easiest answer is to say that, like most other humans, I am hungry. But there is more than that. It seems to me that our three basic needs, for food and security and love, are so mixed and mingled and entwined that we cannot straightly think of one without the others. So it happens that when I write of hunger, I am really writing about love and the hunger for it, and warmth and the love of it and the hunger for it. . . and then it is all one."

➤ In the excerpt from *Serve It Forth*, M. F. K. Fisher uses many words that are likely to be unfamiliar to readers. Describing the eating habits of ancient Egyptians, Fisher sometimes defines a word within the sentence (for example, "spelt, the dried pounded centers of the sacred lotus plants"). Other times she expects the reader to work for the meaning. One might be able to guess at an approximate definition, but for accuracy, you need a dictionary. (*Fellahin*: an Egyptian peasant; *Faience*: brilliantly glazed earthenware or porcelain; *Hetaerae*: literally, companion, but including concubines and courtesans whose charm was increased by a high degree of intelligence and education, making them more agreeable companions than the cloistered Athenian women.)

FOR DISCUSSION AND REFLECTION

➤ Ask students to distinguish among the unfamiliar words they have underlined in the passage. Identify words whose meaning can be understood from context, words that can be guessed at, and words that require the assistance of a dictionary. (Answers will vary, but careful readers can develop their ability to figure out the meaning of unfamiliar words from context.)

➤ What questions does this passage raise in students' minds about eating habits in ancient Egypt? (Responses will vary.)

Writing

QUICK ASSESS

Do students' descriptions:

✔ focus on a particular culture's food habits?

✔ provide a commentary on this culture?

Before students begin to write, have them make a list of words that the members of the group they plan to describe might use but that would be unfamiliar to an outsider. They could use slang, brand names, music references, or other "insider" vocabulary.

READING AND WRITING EXTENSIONS

➤ The first line of M. F. K. Fisher's book *Consider the Oyster* reads, "An oyster leads a dreadful but exciting life." Invite students to use this line for the first sentence of a creative essay of their own, substituting another food for oyster.

➤ Ask students to think of a friend with particular eating habits that seem strange to them. Have students explain what these habits say about this person.

Four Simple Words, Complex Ideas

Critical Reading

BACKGROUND

Margaret Atwood is a Canadian novelist and poet whose works include *The Handmaid's Tale*, *Cat's Eye*, and *Alias Grace*. In "Bread" she examines the possibilities of fiction through the most common of foods. Part one describes the simple act of making a peanut butter and honey sandwich in a kitchen where bread is always present. In part two, she invites the reader to imagine two sisters and one piece of bread in a time of famine. The older sister is faced with the dilemma of eating the bread and saving herself or giving it to her sister who may die of starvation anyway. It ends with the heart-stopping question, "How long does it take you to decide?" Part three asks the reader to imagine a prisoner who is withholding information from his jailers. The piece of bread they have offered him if he talks reminds him of a scene from home and reminds him, too, that the bread "is subversive, it's treacherous, it does not mean life." Part four is adapted from a German fairy tale. A rich sister refuses her poverty-stricken sister the bread she needs to feed her children. When the rich sister's husband cuts himself a piece of the bread that was withheld, the loaf bleeds. Atwood writes, "Everyone knew what that meant," but her meaning is far from clear. In part five, a loaf of bread floats magically above a kitchen table. Atwood describes how the reader, referred to as "you," responds to this vision: "There's no doubt that you can see the bread, you can even smell it, it smells like yeast, and it looks solid enough, solid as your own arm. But can you trust it? Can you eat it? You don't want to know, imagine that."

FOR DISCUSSION AND REFLECTION

➤ Divide the class into five groups. Assign each group a section of "Bread" and ask them to report to the class on their interpretation of Atwood's writing. When all five have been heard, discuss the features that the selections share. (Features may include the focus on bread, the instruction "imagine," the use of the second person to refer to the reader, the use of questions, the simple language, the present tense.)

➤ Ask students to imagine the food that might replace "bread" in another culture. (Responses will vary, but might include, for example, rice in Asian countries.)

Writing

Students are asked to write about the feelings "Bread" evoked in them. Invite them to write tentative interpretations, even beginning sentences with "Maybe . . . ," "It could be that . . .," and "I wonder if . . . ." It may be useful for the class to create a list of puzzling lines and striking images on the board.

READING AND WRITING EXTENSIONS

➤ Margaret Atwood has said that she became a poet one sunny day in high school when a large invisible thumb descended from the sky and pressed down on the top of her head. A poem formed. Invite students to imagine a situation which would inspire them to be a poet.

➤ Have students compose their own part six to "Bread" and then share it with the class.

Five The Power of the Present Tense

Critical Reading

FOCUS

Writers use the present tense in order to bring readers as close as possible to events in the story.

BACKGROUND

The present tense allows readers very little distance from the text. Students should recognize this immediacy as they read Margaret Atwood's "Bread." The action occurs as we read: "She is starving, her belly is bloated, flies land on her eyes; you brush them off with your hand." Writers use the present tense in this manner in order to force readers into a confrontation with the text. It is difficult to escape identifying with the "you."

➤ Only section four, identified as a traditional German fairy tale, is written in the past tense. Here Atwood seems to be saying that horrifying as what she relates may sound, she is only repeating what everyone already knows. Thus it is all the more horrifying.

➤ The use of imperatives, "Imagine a piece of bread . . . a famine . . . a prison," puts the reader in the position of one who must follow directions. The writer is bossing you around, forcing you to do what you otherwise might not want to do. The hard questions the writer keeps asking you have a similar effect: "Should you share the bread or give the whole piece to your sister? Should you eat the piece of bread yourself?" There is something confining about Atwood's text. She does not want the reader to slip out easily.

FOR DISCUSSION AND REFLECTION

➤ Ask students to identify passages from "Bread" that particularly struck or disturbed them. Together, analyze these passages to figure out how Atwood achieved this effect. If students need a prompt, have them analyze, "There is something you know that you have not yet told. Those in control of the prison know that you know. So do those not in control." (Responses will vary.)

➤ What do you like or dislike about Atwood's style? (Responses will vary.)

Writing

QUICK ASSESS

Do students' pieces:

✓ focus on one common, concrete object?

✓ use the present tense and simple language?

✓ imitate Atwood's style and structure?

Students are asked to imitate Atwood's style in a prose piece of their own. With the class, make a list of concrete objects that would be rich subjects for this assignment. Once they have chosen their subjects, have students view their object from various perspectives—for example, from outer space, from the point of view of an ant, at the end of a tunnel, during the Civil War, under the bed, in Paris, and so on.

READING AND WRITING EXTENSIONS

➤ Margaret Atwood was a published poet at age nineteen. An early collection, *The Circle Game*, received the Canadian Governor General's Award for Poetry in 1966. In these and other poetic works, Atwood explores human behavior, celebrates the natural world, and condemns materialism. Bring in a Margaret Atwood poem to share with students and to continue the discussion of her style and word usage.

➤ Research German fairy tales and have each student bring one tale to class to share. Discuss what these stories seem to have in common.

FOCUS ON THE WRITER: JOHN STEINBECK

Unit Overview

In this unit, students will explore the writings and beliefs of John Steinbeck. As they read excerpts from four of his novels and a passage from his 1962 Nobel Prize lecture, students will analyze methods of character development and examine his purpose in writing. Students will discover how knowing about the social issues, beliefs, and values of a writer can enrich their understanding of what they read as they examine Steinbeck's belief in the "perfectibility of man."

Literature Focus

	Lesson	Literature
1.	The Unfinished Children of Nature	from *The Pastures of Heaven* (Novel)
2.	Character Relationships	from *Cannery Row* (Novel)
3.	The Unfinished Child as an Adult	from *Of Mice and Men* (Novel)
4.	Characters as Witnesses	from *The Grapes of Wrath* (Novel)
5.	The Perfectibility of Man	from The Nobel Prize Lecture (Nonfiction)

Reading Focus

1. Description, action, and dialogue all contribute to the development of a believable character.
2. Readers must look beyond the silence of characters to understand their actions.
3. While readers learn about characters through straightforward description and actions, they must also look carefully at the thoughts of the characters themselves.
4. Clear, strongly-defined characters can be effective in persuading people to understand the social or ethical issues dealt with in a novel.
5. Knowing what a writer believes in can help in understanding his or her characters and stories.

Writing Focus

1. Fill out a chart about character development.
2. Write about the relationship between two characters.
3. Analyze a character's feelings, using details from the text.
4. Analyze a character by interpreting the author's description of her.
5. Explain how an author presents the same idea in several works.

One The Unfinished Children of Nature

C r i t i c a l   R e a d i n g

FOCUS

Steinbeck portrayed society's outcasts with sympathy and understanding:

"All of the animals Tularecito had ever seen were there; all the birds of the hills flew above them. . . . There were tomcats and goats, turtles and gophers, every one of them drawn with astonishing detail and veracity."

BACKGROUND

The Pastures of Heaven is an early collection of interrelated stories. In this excerpt, Steinbeck tells the story of Tularecito, a retarded child with a gift for drawing. Gomez, with whom Tularecito lives, says of him, "He can work; he can do marvelous things with his hands, but he cannot learn to do the simple little things of the school. He is not crazy; he is one of those whom God has not quite finished."

➤ In 1931 John Steinbeck wrote to his agent: "There is about twelve miles from Monterey, a valley in the hills called Corral de Tierra. Because I am using its people I have named it Las Pasturas del Cielo. The valley was for years known as the happy valley because of the unique harmony which existed among its twenty families. About ten years ago a new family moved in on one of the ranches. They were ordinary people, ill educated but honest and as kindly as any. In fact, in their whole history I cannot find that they have committed a really malicious act nor an act which was not dictated by honorable expediency or out and out altruism. But about the M___s there was a flavor of evil. Everyone they came in contact with was injured. There have been two murders, a suicide, many quarrels, and a great deal of unhappiness in the Pastures of Heaven, and all these things can be traced to the influence of the M___s. So much is true."

FOR DISCUSSION AND REFLECTION

➤ What do you think is the importance of Miss Martin's statement to Tularecito that "It is a great gift that God has given you"? (She recognizes that Tularecito is a precious being, precious to God if not to other men.)

➤ Ask students to find evidence from the first passage that prepares the reader for the story's devastating conclusion. What details foreshadow that Tularecito will never be able to find a place for himself in the conventional world? (His gift for drawing animals is extraordinary and his passion for defending them obsessive. His manic strength terrifies people.)

W r i t i n g

QUICK ASSESS

Do students' charts:

✔ demonstrate an understanding of Tularecito's behavior?

✔ cite a variety of description, action, and dialogue from Steinbeck's text?

Students are asked to explore their ideas about Tularecito in a chart. Remind students that writers convey information about a character in a variety of ways. For example, what does the simple statement in the fourth paragraph that "Tularecito charged" tell readers about him? (The verb is most commonly applied to a bull, thereby suggesting that there is something animal-like about Tularecito's response.)

READING AND WRITING EXTENSIONS

➤ Ask students to write about how knowing that Tularecito's story is based on a real person influences their attitude toward the character.

➤ Have students think of people who are extraordinarily gifted. Discuss how sometimes these individuals have shortcomings in other areas of their lives.

Two Character Relationships

Critical Reading

FOCUS

Steinbeck believed that people must be seen in the context of their environments:

"There's uncles around all the time at home. Some of them hit me and tell me to get out and some of them give me a nickel and tell me to get out."

BACKGROUND

In this passage from John Steinbeck's *Cannery Row*, students meet Frankie, a character who, like Tularecito, is "one of those whom God has not quite finished." Although Frankie is not wanted either at school or at home, through Doc's help and kindness the boy is able to do menial chores around the laboratory. In return, Doc provides him with food, shelter, and understanding. Frankie adores him.

➤ Doc is an important figure in *Cannery Row* because he serves as the local deity. Like the Greek gods, he mixes freely with ordinary mortals, but his home is in his laboratory, and he is essentially set apart. "Everyone who knew him was indebted to him" and looked up to him for advice and help. These he was always willing and able to give. And no one needed them more than Frankie.

FOR DISCUSSION AND REFLECTION

➤ Reread the first brief exchange of words between Doc and Frankie. Explain Frankie's response to Doc's question, "Don't you ever wash?" (Frankie scrubs his hands because he wants so badly to please Doc. Notice that nowhere has Doc asked him to do so.)

➤ How is what Doc doesn't say to Frankie as important as what he does say in terms of gaining the boy's confidence? (Doc shows that he cares for the boy by his actions rather than his words.)

➤ Compare Frankie with Tularecito. How are the boys alike? How are they different? (Both are cast-offs, unwanted. Both have disabilities. Both find someone who sees good in them—Tularecito has Miss Martin, Frankie has Doc — but even these "saviors" cannot prevent the stories from ending unhappily.)

➤ Do students believe that society has a responsibility to take care of "those whom God has not quite finished"? Why or why not? (Responses will vary.)

Writing

QUICK ASSESS

Do students' responses:

✔ explore their opinions of the quotation?

✔ recognize the complexity of the relationship between Doc and Frankie?

✔ see how Frankie's actions tell the reader what his few words cannot?

As students formulate their opinions on whether or not they agree that "there wasn't a thing in the world he [Doc] could do," ask them to think about a time they tried to please, and it all went wrong. Discuss whether anything could have been done for them.

READING AND WRITING EXTENSIONS

➤ Ask students to write an interior monologue for Frankie as he sits buried in the excelsior box. What thoughts are going through the boy's head?

➤ Encourage studets to read Daniel Keyes's story "Flowers for Algernon" and write about how Charly's relationship with his teacher is very like Frankie's with Doc.

Three The Unfinished Child as an Adult

Critical Reading

FOCUS

John Steinbeck once remarked that his goal as a writer of fiction was "to cut up reality and make it more real."

BACKGROUND

Clinging to each other in their loneliness, George and his simple-minded friend Lennie dream of a place to call their own. But after they come to work on a ranch in the Salinas Valley, their hopes, like "the best laid schemes o' mice an' men," begin to go awry. The Robert Burns poem from which the novel takes its title laments man's enslavement to forces of nature that he cannot control and that relentlessly but indifferently destroy his ambitions and illusions. The dream of the farm originates with Lennie, and it is only through Lennie, who also makes the dream impossible, that the dream has any meaning for George.

➤ Help students recognize that almost every character in the story asks George why he hangs around with Lennie. George's answers vary from outright lies to the simple statement, "We travel together." It is only to Slim, the superior workman with "God-like eyes," that he tells the truth. Among several reasons, such as his feeling of responsibility for Lennie in return for the latter's unfailing loyalty and their having grown up together, there is another: "He's dumb as hell, but he ain't crazy. An' I ain't so bright neither, or I wouldn't be buckin' barley for my fifty and found." George needs Lennie as much as Lennie needs George.

FOR DISCUSSION AND REFLECTION

➤ Ask students who Lennie is talking to in this passage. (He speaks largely to himself, though some of his remarks are aimed at the dead puppy.)

➤ What does this reveal about Lennie and Lennie's relationship with the world? (Like a child, he talks to the world, asking it to answer for itself: "Why do you got to get killed?")

Writing

QUICK ASSESS

Do students' explanations:

✔ recognize the various strategies John Steinbeck uses to reveal Lennie's character?

✔ see how a reader's interpretation of events may differ from a character's account of these events?

Before students attempt to explain the strategies Steinbeck employs in order to make a reader feel Lennie's remorse, ask them to underline words or phrases in the passage that indicate Lennie's state of mind. Then begin to categorize these examples in terms of literary technique.

READING AND WRITING EXTENSIONS

➤ Ask students to write a dialogue between George and Lennie that they think might take place when George returns and finds Lennie in the barn.

➤ Watch this scene from the movie *Of Mice and Men*. Have students discuss whether John Malkovich's portrayal of Lennie matched their interpretation of the character.

Four Characters as Witnesses

Critical Reading

FOCUS

John Steinbeck's *The Grapes of Wrath* won the 1940 Pulitzer Prize and is his most widely read and admired work.

BACKGROUND

The Grapes of Wrath is a controversial classic because it is at once populist and revolutionary. It advances a belief in the essential goodness and forbearance of the "common people" and prophesies a fundamental change to produce equitable social conditions: "There is a crime here that goes beyond denunciation. There is a sorrow here that weeping cannot symbolize. There is failure here that topples all our success … in the eyes of the hungry there is a growing wrath. In the soul of the people the grapes of wrath are filling and growing heavy, growing heavy for the vintage." (Chapter 25)

➤ Ma Joad is the true leader of the Joad family, keeping it together under the most trying of circumstances. Following the ways of her people, she subordinates herself to Pa Joad and at the beginning of the novel has little to say at the family council. She is its anchor, though, because she knows "that if she swayed the family shook, and if she ever really deeply wavered or despaired the family would fall."

FOR DISCUSSION AND REFLECTION

➤ What does Steinbeck mean when he calls Ma Joad "the citadel of the family"? (Literally a citadel is a fortress overlooking a city. Steinbeck portrays Ma Joad as the family's protector and source of strength.)

➤ Explain the metaphor Steinbeck employs when he says it was Ma Joad's habit "to build up laughter out of inadequate materials." (Though often there was little to laugh about in the Joads' lives, Ma found ways to squeeze happiness out of what there was.)

Writing

QUICK ASSESS

Do students' interpretations:

✔ reflect a careful reading of the text?

✔ use specific evidence from the passage to support their opinion?

✔ demonstrate an understanding of Steinbeck's methods of revealing character?

Before students begin to write their responses, have them create a list on the board of possible interpretations of the line "Then she knew."

READING AND WRITING EXTENSIONS

➤ John Steinbeck in a 1939 NBC radio program:

"Boileau said that kings, gods, and heroes only were fit subjects for literature. The writer can only write about what he admires. Present-day kings aren't very inspiring, the gods are on a vacation and about the only heroes left are the scientists and the poor. . . . But the poor are still in the open. When they make a struggle it is an heroic struggle with starvation, death or imprisonment the penalty if they lose. And since our race admires gallantry, the writer will deal with it where he finds it. He finds it in the struggling poor now."

Read the above passage to students and discuss how Ma Joad fits Steinbeck's description of a "struggling poor" hero.

➤ Have students write a poem in praise of Ma Joad.

Five The Perfectibility of Man

C r i t i c a l   R e a d i n g

FOCUS

John Steinbeck on what writers believe:

"I hold that a writer who does not passionately believe in the perfectibility of man has no dedication nor any membership in literature."

BACKGROUND

Only five other Americans had won the Nobel Prize for Literature before John Steinbeck: Sinclair Lewis, Eugene O'Neill, Pearl Buck, William Faulkner, and Ernest Hemingway. Although Steinbeck had scoffed at the meaning and significance of the prize in earlier years, describing it as the equivalent of a writer's funeral service, he was very proud to receive it. Steinbeck's Nobel speech was a valediction. It is at once humble in its tone, graceful in its word choice, and moralistic in its message. In short, the speech was a microcosm of Steinbeck's life work.

FOR DISCUSSION AND REFLECTION

➤ What roles do writers play in society today? Do these roles carry responsibilities? (Responses will vary, but consider a variety of writers: journalists, novelists, scriptwriters, poets, speech writers, television writers, textbook writers, advertising copywriters, and so on.)

➤ Are writers, as Steinbeck says in his Nobel speech, "delegated to declare and to celebrate man's proven capacity for greatness of heart and spirit — for gallantry in defeat, for courage, compassion and love"? (Responses will vary.)

➤ What do you think Steinbeck means when he says he believes in the "perfectibility of man"? (That with dedicated effort, human beings can behave better than they have thus far in history. That evil need not triumph in the world. That injustice can be eradicated, and fairness someday triumph.)

➤ Ask students if they believe that man is "perfectible." Is it possible to believe that people will always be rogues and yet continue to work to improve the lives of those around you? (Responses will vary.)

W r i t i n g

QUICK ASSESS

Do students' explanations:

✓ show how Steinbeck demonstrates what he believes in through the vehicle of his characters?

✓ refer to a variety of novels?

As students formulate their explanation of Steinbeck's belief in the perfectibility of man, urge them to reread the passages from his novels. It may help students to be reminded that they are looking for evidence of individuals who through their actions make this world a slightly better place for those around them.

READING AND WRITING EXTENSIONS

➤ Read a dictonary's definition of the word "perfect." Then have students use this definition as a starting point to write a dialogue between a man and a woman who are having an argument over what constitutes a "perfect" man or woman. The two need not come to agreement.

➤ Invite students to imagine that John Steinbeck will be visiting their school next week. Make a class list of questions they would like to ask him about his work and his ideas. Then have students take on the role of Steinbeck to answer the questions in a series of short interviews.

U n i t   O v e r v i e w

"Essentials of Reading" invites students to explore five essentials of the reading process: making predictions, understanding the main idea, drawing inferences, rereading effectively, and identifying the writer's purpose. By responding to a variety of fiction and nonfiction, students will develop their abilities to read actively.

L i t e r a t u r e   F o c u s

Lesson	Literature
1. Thinking With the Writer	**Kate Chopin,** "The Story of an Hour" (Short Story)
2. Considering the Theme	
3. Reading Between the Lines	**Jane Smiley,** from *A Thousand Acres* (Novel)
4. Doubling Back	
5. Author's Purpose	**Steve Wulf,** "A Flower in the Outfield" (Nonfiction)

R e a d i n g   F o c u s

1. Active readers make predictions as they read. Most of the predictions are about what will happen or what characters are like.

2. Critical readers know that finding the main idea is an essential part of reading. In fiction, character and plot descriptions can provide valuable clues about the main idea.

3. It is important to make inferences about what the author is saying. These inferences will improve your understanding of a work's characters, plot, and setting.

4. Multiple readings of a text are generally necessary before you can focus on elements of an author's style and language.

5. Understanding an author's purpose or intent is an essential part of reading. Many times the organization, style, and tone of a piece can provide clues to the author's intent.

W r i t i n g   F o c u s

1. Extend a story based on predictions about what will happen next.

2. Explain the main idea of a story, using quotations to support the interpretation.

3. Write a one-paragraph introduction to an excerpt from a novel, including information about character, plot, and setting.

4. Answer several questions that explore how rereading enhances the understanding of style, language, and tone.

5. Write a letter to the editor that critiques the author's ideas and purpose.

One Thinking With the Writer

Critical Reading

FOCUS

As a story unfolds, active readers make predictions about what is likely to happen next.

BACKGROUND

As they read Kate Chopin's "The Story of an Hour" and answer the prediction questions, encourage students to think about what details in the text have led them to those predictions.

➤ Kate Chopin (1851–1904) was the well-bred daughter of a wealthy St. Louis family. Victorian values and a Catholic education were her preparation for marriage to Oscar Chopin, a Creole cotton trader. On the surface, she was a happy and dutiful wife as well as the devoted mother of six children. When her husband died of swamp fever in 1883, the bereaved Kate was said to be "inconsolable." Oscar Chopin's death thrust his widow into a new life of reading, including such modern writers as Charles Darwin, Guy de Maupassant, and Gustave Flaubert. Kate Chopin also began to write. Many of her early stories examine the inequities of conventional marriage.

➤ Stopping to jot down what will happen next may seem artificial, as active readers engage in prediction all the time. Yet, it is valuable for all readers to become aware of the strategies they use to move through a story.

FOR DISCUSSION AND REFLECTION

➤ Why was Louise able to come to terms with her husband's death? (She saw with his death would come new freedom. The "something coming to her" is the awareness of "a long procession of years to come that would belong to her absolutely; she would live for herself.")

➤ What is ironic about the ending of this story? (The doctors said that "she had died of heart disease — of joy that kills," but the reader and the narrator know what the characters do not. Mrs. Mallory has died not from happiness but from despair.)

Writing

QUICK ASSESS

Do students' narratives:

✔ offer reasonable predictions based on textual details?

✔ reflect an awareness of the author's style?

Have students characterize Kate Chopin's style before they attempt to imitate it.

READING AND WRITING EXTENSIONS

➤ When Kate Chopin's novel *The Awakening* was published in 1899, critics assailed it as "sad and mad and bad." Like "The Story of an Hour" the novel explores a late-nineteenth century woman's growth toward sexual and emotional independence. The book and Kate Chopin's reputation as a writer languished in oblivion until the 1960s when feminist critics rediscovered her work. Invite students to speculate why the message of "The Story of an Hour" might have particular significance for people interested in re-examining the roles of men and women.

➤ Ask students to think about a time when they received a shocking surprise. Have them describe how they felt mentally and physically.

Two Considering the Theme

Critical Reading

FOCUS

By Sven Birkerts in *Literature, The Evolving Canon:*

"Themes are the understandings we reach when we look searchingly at the most important parts of the human experience. They are, for this simple reason, universal, covering the primary emotions and relations: love, hate, friendship, betrayal, loss, fear, idealism, and on and on. We find them in stories and novels because we find them in our lives. They cannot be taken care of once and for all; they can only be explored."

BACKGROUND

If characters, plot, and setting make up the body of a work of literature, the theme is its heart. The author's generalization about life, the theme is often the thing that drives an author to write in the first place. But however central theme is to fiction, it is often difficult to pin down.

➤ As students reread "The Story of an Hour," they may feel overwhelmed at the prospect of having to figure out the theme. Assure them that they are engaged in an interpretive process and not the hunt for one perfect generalization to stand in place of the text. Help them see that the theme does more than identify the subject; it makes a generalization about that subject.

FOR DISCUSSION AND REFLECTION

➤ How does the title, "The Story of an Hour," offer readers insight into Chopin's theme? (Within a very short period of time Mrs. Mallory is told of her husband's death, begins to grieve, realizes that with this death will come new-found freedom, exalts in the possibilities that lie ahead, sees her husband alive, and dies. It could be said that this particular hour represents the story of Mrs. Mallory's whole life.)

➤ What lines and passages from the story provide insights into the author's ideas about the subject? (Responses will vary but should include descriptions of Louise's changing emotions.)

➤ Ask students to think about Sven Birkerts's explanation of theme as they listen to one another's interpretations of Kate Chopin's theme in "The Story of an Hour."

Writing

QUICK ASSESS

Do students' interpretations:

✓ reflect careful reading?

✓ identify the theme?

✓ use quotations from the story as support?

Warn students that bald statements of a theme ("A loving marriage is sometimes a prison" or "Without freedom there can be no life" or "Victorian marriages kept women confined") in no way convey the richness of the story. Students should make tentative approximations of Chopin's themes, supporting their hunches with evidence, but also remain open to other readers' interpretations. There is no one right answer here.

READING AND WRITING EXTENSIONS

➤ Imagine that Mr. Mallory had died in the accident. Ask students to describe how Mrs. Mallory's life would have changed.

➤ Women's roles have changed a great deal since Kate Chopin wrote "The Story of an Hour." Discuss with students whether this means that the story is dated and without significance to contemporary readers or whether the story still has something important to say to us.

Three Reading Between the Lines

Critical Reading

FOCUS

In order to "read between the lines," readers must make inferences and draw conclusions from story details.

BACKGROUND

Jane Smiley says that she had "four or five" ideas for her novel *A Thousand Acres* that she felt were related: big American farms, relationships within a dysfunctional family, linking the exploitation of the environment with that of women, and *King Lear*.

➤ Students will need to "read between the lines" in order to determine Smiley's characters, plot, and setting in this passage from early in the novel. For example, consider this sentence: "No globe or map fully convinced me that Zebulon County was not the center of the universe." A reader can infer from it that the adult narrator realizes that for her 8-year-old self the family farm (and the father who personified these thousand acres) was the world. The narrator goes on to explain how the people in her life — neighbors and friends — were identified by their relationship to the land: "The Ericsons had three hundred acres and a mortgage." Even the car from which she views the landscape is defined in acreage: "The car was the exact measure of six hundred forty acres compared to three hundred or five hundred." An active reader will begin to realize that this is the way the young girl sees the world and start to look for how this shapes her view in the fictional world.

FOR DISCUSSION AND REFLECTION

➤ Ask students to point out details in the passage that can be interpreted as evidence of a happy, secure childhood. (Possible responses include the pies and doughnuts, Sunday dinners, the "velvet luxury of the car's interior," the "reassuring note of my father's and mother's voices" described as a duet, the imposing and well cared for farm buildings, "our farm and our lives seemed secure and good.")

➤ Is there any evidence to suggest that this picture of well-being may shatter? (The narrator describes the parents as "complacent." Looking back, she realizes that "they had probably seen nearly as little of the world as I had by that time." Stories revolve around conflict. This idyllic picture of the narrator's childhood is the ground upon which the rest of the story is built.)

Writing

QUICK ASSESS

Do students' introductions:

✔ include information about character, plot, and setting?

✔ reflect reasonable conclusions drawn from the details of Smiley's writing?

Students are asked to write an introduction to the excerpt from Smiley's book that includes information about the character, plot, and setting. Remind students that some of their information will be based upon inferences.

READING AND WRITING EXTENSIONS

➤ Many of Jane Smiley's stories begin with the description of what appears to be an idyllic life in a pastoral setting. Ask students to write a story of their own that begins in this manner.

➤ Encourage students to think back to the time when their view of the world was identical to that of their parents. Have them write about how this has changed as they have grown older. What do they think caused the change?

Four Doubling Back

Critical Reading

FOCUS

Rereading allows us to pay careful attention to a writer's style.

BACKGROUND

The greatest advantage teachers as readers have over their students as readers is that we have often read the piece of literature under discussion many, many times. As a result, features of a text which seem obvious to the instructor are often invisible to students. One way to help students "see" is to have them reread the text. But unless teachers give students a new task to accomplish during this second time through the text, only a few are likely to comply.

➤ This lesson asks students to reread the excerpt from *A Thousand Acres* and underline words or passages that reflect Jane Smiley's writing style, language, and tone. Help them get started by indicating places in the text that you would mark. If available, highlighters can be useful tools. For example, ask students to take one paragraph and make a mark wherever they see a period in order to draw attention to comparative sentence length.

FOR DISCUSSION AND REFLECTION

➤ How do the short sentences, "A thousand acres. It was that simple," affect you as a reader? (They punctuate the paragraph and draw attention to its main idea.)

➤ Read aloud the long sentence in the sixth paragraph that begins "For me it was a pleasure . . ." and ask students to speculate on why Smiley might have chosen to layer image upon image in this manner. Is she purposely making things difficult for her readers? (In a way, yes. The writer wants the reader to hesitate, reflect, reread.)

➤ Discuss the tone of this passage. When students offer generalizations, ask them to back these up with specific lines from the text.

Writing

QUICK ASSESS

Are students' descriptions:

✓ based on specific references to the text?

✓ accurate and complete?

In a prewriting activity, students are asked to read Smiley's story excerpt a second time, paying special attention to her style, language, and tone. Then they summarize their observations in three brief descriptive paragraphs.

READING AND WRITING EXTENSIONS

➤ "True ease in writing comes from art not chance
As those move easiest who have learned to dance.
'Tis not enough no harshness gives offense
The sound must seem an echo to the sense." (Alexander Pope)

How is the sound of Jane Smiley's sentences an "echo to the sense" she conveys?

➤ Ask students to think of a story that they enjoyed reading or having read to them over and over again as a child. Discuss why these stories did not seem to grow stale with rereading.

Five Author's Purpose

Critical Reading

FOCUS

From Holman and Harmon's *A Handbook to Literature*:

"The personal essay is a kind of informal essay with an intimate style, some autobiographical content or interest, and an urbane conversational manner."

BACKGROUND

The personal essay is distinguished from the formal essay by its friendly, conversational tone, its candor, and its often quirky first-person voice. Frequently humorous, it is perhaps the most approachable and diverting type of nonfiction. Steve Wulf's "A Flower in the Outfield" is an excellent example of the genre. In it the writer describes a Little League season that was on one level a complete disaster and on another a glorious success.

FOR DISCUSSION AND REFLECTION

➤ Reread the opening and closing paragraphs of Wulf's essay. How does the writer return to a familiar image in his conclusion? (The statement "We were yellow" would typically have the negative connotation of cowardice, but for this plucky team in yellow uniforms, "One big yellow flower bloomed in the outfield that day.")

➤ What does the writer mean by "Let's hope it's a perennial, even if only in their memory"? (Whether or not the joys of this baseball season are repeated in future years, he hopes that the boys will look back on what they achieved together with pride and pleasure.)

➤ Why do you think Steve Wulf wrote this piece? (as a way to record and remember the season, as a way to understand what he experienced as a coach, as a tribute to the players, as a fresh take on the cliché that winning isn't everything)

➤ How would you characterize Wulf's attitude toward the Little Leaguers on his team? (extreme fondness: "We led the league in tears," "This was the nicest group of kids either one of us had ever coached.")

Writing

QUICK ASSESS

Do students' letters:

✓ have the mechanical correctness necessary to be taken seriously?

✓ demonstrate a clear understanding of Wulf's purpose?

✓ contain specific references to Wulf's column?

After completing a mini-worksheet about Wulf's piece, students are asked to critique the essay in a letter to the editor. As students begin, suggest that they think about a time when they played on a losing team or about a coach they remember. Another possibility would be to have them agree or disagree with Wulf's premise that winning isn't everything.

READING AND WRITING EXTENSIONS

➤ In his introduction to the anthology *The Art of the Personal Essay,* Phillip Lopate writes, "The hallmark of the personal essay is its intimacy. The writer seems to be speaking directly into your ear, confiding everything from gossip to wisdom. Through sharing thoughts, memories, desires, complaints, and whimsies, the personal essayist sets up a relationship with the reader, a dialogue — a friendship, if you will, based on identification, understanding, testiness, and companionship." To what extent do students feel "A Flower in the Outfield" achieved what Lopate describes?

➤ Have students write a personal essay about a seemingly awful experience that turned out to have, if not a happy ending, at least a bittersweet one.

STORIES THROUGH THE AGES

Unit Overview

In "Stories Through the Ages," students will consider the ways in which fables and folk tales use animal characters to comment on human behavior. As they explore personification, learn about trickster figures, and write their own fables, students will discover the cultural context of a variety of animal stories.

Literature Focus

	Lesson	Literature
1.	Lessons in Animal Fables	"The Monkey and the Crocodile" (Folk Tale)
2.	Fables in Cultural Context	"The Hawk and the Buzzard" (Folk Tale)
3.	Personification in Fables	"No Tracks Coming Back" (Folk Tale)
4.	Characteristics of Tricksters	"Anansi and His Visitor, Turtle" (Folk Tale)
5.	Stories of Animals Today	**Terry Tempest Williams,** "Peregrine Falcon" from *Refuge* (Nonfiction)

Reading Focus

1. Fables are stories that teach lessons about human concerns, traits, and actions.
2. Because fables are common to all cultures, they highlight the unique aspects and ideas of each culture.
3. The lessons taught in fables vary from simple morals to complex statements about how we live. Even as they entertain, fables are still critiquing human nature.
4. The trickster is a unique character in stories, personifying many of the darker aspects of human nature, but doing so with humor and wit.
5. Writers still link stories about the animal world with human behavior, even if these stories are not fables.

Writing Focus

1. Write a paragraph that explains the lesson of a fable.
2. Write a contemporary animal fable based on current situations in the news or in your own life.
3. Create a fable in which a cunning animal outsmarts a stronger opponent.
4. Extend a fable by writing another episode with the same trickster characters.
5. Explore how a naturalist's observations relate to human nature and human society.

One Lessons in Animal Fables

Critical Reading

FOCUS

A fable differs from the ordinary folk tale in that it has a moral woven into the story and animals illustrate human traits.

BACKGROUND

A fable is a story of supernatural or marvelous happenings. Fables typically convey useful truths. Traditionally quite short, these instructive stories have as their main characters animals who speak like human beings. Many fables offer advice about the best way to deal with the competitive realities of life. "The Monkey and the Crocodile" is one such tale.

➤ In this Indian fable a greedy little monkey outsmarts a big, foolish crocodile. Point out that the writer uses capital letters for the words *Monkey* and *Crocodile* because an animal's species also serves as his character name.

FOR DISCUSSION AND REFLECTION

➤ Where does the storyteller foreshadow early in the fable the outcome of Monkey and Crocodile's encounter? (Though Crocodile's mother told him to "Put your wits to work," he "was a stupid Crocodile.")

➤ Identify the places in the fable where Crocodile demonstrates his stupidity. (He tells Monkey that he plans to kill him for his heart. He doesn't know that Monkey can't possibly have "left his heart back there in the tree.")

➤ How does the monkey's greed almost get him into trouble? (By asking the crocodile to take him to the tree with the fruit before going back for his heart, Monkey gives Crocodile a chance to figure out Monkey's stratagem or for someone else to "wise Crocodile up.")

➤ How do the physical differences between these two animals contribute to the success of the fable? (The quick-moving monkey is also quick-witted. The languorous crocodile, though much the monkey's physical superior, can never quite catch up with him.)

Writing

QUICK ASSESS

Do students' explanations:

✔ identify the lesson within a fable?

✔ use specific evidence from the story as support?

Students are asked to explain what they think is the general lesson to be learned from this fable. Remind them that the lessons in a fable are intended for people and should be expressed in terms of human behavior.

READING AND WRITING EXTENSIONS

➤ Vikram Seth, a contemporary Indian author, has written an updated collection of animal stories called *Beastly Tales*. Read Seth's lively, rhyming version of this tale aloud to students and ask them to compare the two.

➤ Invite students to imagine themselves as an animal whose traits match their own and then to imagine someone whom they often find themselves in conflict with as their antagonist. Write a story about one of these conflicts set in the animal kingdom.

Two Fables in Cultural Context

Critical Reading

FOCUS

Julius Lester on folklore:

"The authentic folktale can never be restricted to its place of cultural or geographical origin. By definition, the folktale partakes of the universal."

BACKGROUND

Humans create folk tales because it is in these tales that we communicate our fears, our hopes, and our dreams. It is in story that we seek to understand the whys and hows of our world and ourselves. As Julius Lester writes in his introduction to *Black Folktales*, "We do not believe the tale literally, but we trust its heart. We know that the tale speaks a truth, but it is an elusive truth, a truth that can never be wholly put into words."

➤ "The Hawk and the Buzzard" is a tale collected by Zora Neale Hurston in the 1930s. Hurston believed that folklore is the art people create before they find out there is such a thing as art; it comes from a folk's "first wondering contact with natural law."

➤ In *Mules and Men*, Zora Neale Hurston wrote that "From the earliest rocking of my cradle, I had known about the capers Brer Rabbit is apt to cut and what the Squinch Owl says from the house top. But it was fitting me like a tight chemise. I couldn't see it for wearing it. It was only when I was off in college, away from my native surroundings, that I could see myself like somebody else and stand off and look at my garment. Then I had to have the spy-glass of Anthropology to look through at that."

FOR DISCUSSION AND REFLECTION

➤ What do students know about the natural habits of buzzards and hawks? (They need to know that buzzards feed on carcasses in order to make sense of this folk tale.)

➤ What qualities do you associate with a hawk? (glorious flight, nobility, a fearsome predator)

➤ What qualities do you associate with a buzzard? (a harbinger and sign of death and decay, a scavenger)

➤ What natural law would you say this tale of "The Hawk and the Buzzard" explores? (Different species have different purposes in this world, and while some like the hawk seem to get all the glory, others like the buzzard will "live to pick yo' bones.")

Writing

QUICK ASSESS

Do students' fables:

✓ pose a conflict through animal traits?

✓ offer a clear lesson?

Before students construct their fables, have them discuss their ideas about the lesson in "The Hawk and the Buzzard" and brainstorm ideas based on current events.

READING AND WRITING EXTENSIONS

➤ Invite students to share the stories that they currently wear in what Zora Neale Hurston refers to as "a tight chemise."

➤ Discuss the possible reasons why slaves may have used animal tales to teach their children about life.

Three Personification in Fables

Critical Reading

FOCUS

Personification is a figure of speech in which human characteristics are attributed to animals, abstract qualities, or inanimate objects.

BACKGROUND

In animal fables, personification allows readers to reflect upon human foibles without feeling as though we are being scolded. Because the stories of talking animals could not possibly be true, we allow the storyteller the creative leeway to craft a tale that, in fact, teaches us something we need to know. Nobody likes a didactic lecture. Everybody loves a good story.

➤ In "No Tracks Coming Back," clever Brer Rabbit, the trickster in African American folk tales, avoids Brer Fox's trap. Though the fox is a natural predator of the rabbit and has evidently been able to lure many furry creatures to his "big meeting," Brer Rabbit outsmarts his foe and lives to tell the tale.

FOR DISCUSSION AND REFLECTION

➤ Ask students to recount in their own words what happens in this short tale. (Brer Rabbit meets Brer Fox along the road. Brer Fox asks if he's going to the big meeting with the other animals. Brer Rabbit tells Brer Fox yes, but when he notices that hundreds of rabbit tracks lead into the meeting place but none lead out, he changes his mind: "Dat ain't no place fo' me.")

➤ What is the lesson to be learned from the fable "No Tracks Coming Back"? (Think before you act. Pay attention to the signs that are there for you to see.)

➤ Have students circle the verbs used in the fable and ask them to explain how these contribute to the personification of the animals. (Consider, for example, "Brer Rabbit was walking along.")

Writing

QUICK ASSESS

Do students' fables:

✔ use personification effectively?

✔ create contrasting characteristics in animals to teach a lesson?

Before they begin to write their own, have students look back at the three fables they have read. Point out how a powerful natural tension is created in each through the animals' contrasting physical characteristics. Recommend that student writers imitate this feature in their fables. Make a list of interesting combinations on the board to help students get started.

READING AND WRITING EXTENSIONS

➤ The Western tradition of the fable began in Greece with tales ascribed to Aesop, almost certainly a legendary figure. Read students Aesop's "The Donkey and the Lap-Dog," "The Frog and the Ox," or "The Bee and the Dove," and ask them to explain how the contrasting features of the animals contribute to the fable's effect.

➤ Have students think of something that adults typically teach children (to floss their teeth, never to smoke cigarettes, call if they'll be late, to buckle their seatbelts) and write a modern animal fable that teaches this lesson.

Four Characteristics of Tricksters

Critical Reading

FOCUS

From *Merriam Webster's Encyclopedia of Literature:*

"A trickster is a mischievous supernatural being much given to capricious acts of sly deception."

BACKGROUND

The trickster appears in the literature of every culture. He is cunning personified, yet his tendency to meddle in things about which he lacks knowledge causes him to make a fool of himself with great regularity. He is subversive in that he crosses forbidden territory, but trickster has no admirable reason for doing so. He lies, he cheats, he steals, but always without malice and often to his own detriment.

➤ In most African cycles the trickster is an underdog figure, smaller in stature and strength than his opponent but much cleverer and always well in control of the situation. He is ruthless, greedy, a glutton, and often outwits his opponent through a calculating shrewdness combined with a complete lack of scruples.

➤ In the folk tale "Anansi and His Visitor, Turtle," two traditional West African trickster characters attempt to get the best of each other. When Anansi the spider tricks Turtle out of a meal in his house by sending him over and over again to the stream to wash until the food is all gone, Turtle devises a plan to return the favor.

FOR DISCUSSION AND REFLECTION

➤ Why do you think West African tricksters, in this case Anansi the spider and Turtle, are often small in stature and strength? (gains the audience's sympathy)

➤ What is the message of this fable? (Though you may get the best of someone once, a clever man will exact his revenge. No matter how smart you are, usually someone out there is smarter.)

Writing

QUICK ASSESS

Do students' episodes:

✓ identify the defining features of a trickster?

✓ maintain the original characterization of Anansi and Turtle?

✓ offer a lesson?

Before students are asked to write an additional episode of the Anansi and Turtle story, mention that fables are wonderfully visual stories. As a prewriting activity, invite students to draw a storyboard of what they plan to write about Anansi and Turtle's next adventure.

READING AND WRITING EXTENSIONS

➤ *Zomo the Rabbit,* a children's picture book by Gerald McDermott, is another trickster tale from West Africa. The opening lines define Zomo perfectly: "He is not big. He is not strong. But he is very clever!" Read the story aloud and ask students what they think might happen if Zomo showed up at Anansi's house for dinner one evening.

➤ Ask students if they see themselves as tricksters or more commonly as those who get tricked. Have them write about why they think this is so.

Five Stories of Animals Today

Critical Reading

FOCUS

From *Refuge*, by Terry Tempest Williams:

"I am not contemplating starlings. It is the falcon I wait for—the duckhawk with a memory for birds that once blotted out the sun."

BACKGROUND

Terry Tempest Williams is the naturalist-in-residence at the Utah Museum of Natural History in Salt Lake City. Her book, *Refuge: An Unnatural History of Family and Place*, tells of how the Great Salt Lake rose to record levels and eventually flooded the wetlands that serve as a refuge for migratory birds in Northern Utah. Williams tells the story against the backdrop of her family's struggle with cancer as a result of living downwind from a nuclear test site.

➤ In this excerpt from *Refuge*, Williams makes a comparison between the thousands of starlings thriving at the Salt Lake City municipal dump and the one peregrine falcon that has managed to survive. Williams characterizes the starlings as "sophisticated mimics," liars, greedy birds who, like man, "are taking over the world."

FOR DISCUSSION AND REFLECTION

➤ What is the tone of "Peregrine Falcon"? (It is self-deprecatory. Williams is able to laugh at her own fondness for sitting on Hefty bags in a trash dump counting birds. Like the animal fables students have read, this essay is far from a boring lecture on birds. It entertains as well as teaches.)

➤ Ask students to point out places in the text that indicate Williams's powers of observation. (Responses will vary.)

➤ In a radio interview with Scott London in 1995, Williams said, "I worry that we are a people in a process of great transition and we are forgetting what we are connected to. We are losing our frame of reference. Pelicans pass by and we hardly know who they are, we don't know their stories. At what price? I think it's leading us to a place of inconsolable loneliness." Ask students if they agree or disagree with Williams. Is our separation from the natural world and our attraction to the material and mechanical worlds dangerous? (Responses will vary.)

Writing

QUICK ASSESS

Do students' answers:

✓ explore the comparison Williams draws between starlings and humans?

✓ focus on the author's lessons about our endangered environment?

As students write about the lessons they learned from Terry Tempest Williams's essay, invite them to think about how these lessons are different from the lessons of traditional fables. Mention that Williams uses the Christmas Bird Count and the natural adaptation of animals to the unnatural effects of progress as a means of warning readers about the dangers of becoming disconnected from our environment. What will we have lost when the last Peregrine Falcon dies?

READING AND WRITING EXTENSIONS

➤ Terry Tempest Williams uses strikingly poetic language in her essay. Have students underline words and phrases that they found appealing for their beauty or imagery. Then have students rearrange these lines into a found poem. If one phrase is particularly striking, they may choose to repeat it.

➤ Ask students to write a letter to Terry Tempest Williams telling her how they feel about the relationship between economic progress and our environment.

TRANSFORMING STORIES

Unit Overview

In this unit, students will explore the ways in which writers retell older stories by changing elements such as point of view, setting, time period, and theme. In "Transforming Stories," students will read and respond to a short story and poetic versions of a biblical story and a traditional fairy tale.

Literature Focus

Lesson	Literature
1. The Changing Story	**Gabriel García Márquez,** "The Handsomest Drowned Man in the World" (Short Story)
2. Recasting a Story	
3. Reinterpretations	**Anna Akhmatova,** "Lot's Wife" (Poetry) Genesis, 19:12-26 (Biblical Text)
4. Timeless Stories	
5. Changing Perspectives	**Randall Jarrell,** "Jack" (Poetry)

Reading Focus

1. Stories evolve over time. They reflect the questions and challenges that various people face and how those are interpreted.
2. Recasting a story into a form and language of one's own is a way of interpreting and understanding stories.
3. Stories build on other stories. Writers often retell and reinterpret older stories to emphasize different perspectives and ideas.
4. The same story will have different meanings and interpretations at different times in history.
5. Changes in perspective are another way of transforming older stories. These versions may change time period, speaker, setting, emphasis, or the moral of the story.

Writing Focus

1. Examine how characters in a short story create their own story.
2. Recast a short story into song lyrics.
3. Write a paragraph that analyzes a poet's transformation of a biblical story.
4. Write two paragraphs—one that explains how information about the poet's life affects your reading of a poem and one that explores how a story connects with your life.
5. Change the perspective of a fairy tale to create a new version.

One The Changing Story

Critical Reading

FOCUS

Stories reflect the values and beliefs of a culture.

BACKGROUND

Gabriel García Márquez is a central figure in the magical realism movement in Latin American literature. The literary phenomenon magical realism is characterized by the incorporation of fantastic or mythical elements matter-of-factly into otherwise realistic fiction. Born in Aracataca, Colombia, the inspiration for the fictional Macondo of *One Hundred Years of Solitude,* García Márquez worked for more than a decade as a journalist in Latin America and Europe before becoming a novelist and short story writer. He is recognized as a master storyteller of epic proportions.

➤ In an interview for *Paris Review* García Márquez said, "It always amuses me that the biggest praise for my work comes for the imagination while the truth is that there's not a single line in all my work that does not have a basis in reality. The problem is that Latin American reality resembles the wildest imagination."

FOR DISCUSSION AND REFLECTION

➤ How does the juxtaposition of the words "handsomest" and "drowned" in the title prepare the reader for the kind of story this is going to be? (It seems a contradiction that a drowned man should be handsome. Márquez is preparing the reader for the surprising occurrences which follow.)

➤ What is unexpected about the townspeople's response to the corpse? (Instead of being repulsed by it, they are attracted to the body and find themselves wanting to care for it.)

➤ How did the presence of the drowned man in the village improve people's lives? ("But they also knew that everything would be different from then on, that their houses would have wider doors, higher ceilings, and stronger floors so that Esteban's memory could go everywhere...." He enlarged their lives, made their community a place that others would point to and say, "Yes, over there, that's Esteban's village.")

Writing

QUICK ASSESS

Do students' sentences:

✓ demonstrate understanding of the plot?

✓ clarify how the villagers begin to sympathize with the corpse?

✓ explain how the villagers take an event and weave it into a myth?

Before students comment on the factors that contribute to the transformation of the corpse into Esteban, remind them to use the actions of the villagers as a guide to understanding the story that evolves.

READING AND WRITING EXTENSIONS

➤ The people of the village respond to the presence of a handsome drowned man in their midst in distinctly different ways. Have students imagine themselves first as a child who found the body on the shore, then a wife, and then one of the fishermen. Write an interior monologue of what each would be thinking that night before falling asleep.

➤ Students love to imitate magical realist stories. Invite them to write their own version of García Márquez's story called, for example: "The Ugliest Miss America," "The Clumsiest Pickpocket in the City," "The Happiest Sad Man in the World," or "The Slowest Sprinter on the Team."

TwoRecasting a Story

Critical Reading

FOCUS

From Gabriel García Márquez's 1982 Nobel Prize Lecture:

"Poets and beggars, musicians and prophets, warriors and scoundrels, all creatures of that unbridled reality, we have had to ask but little of imagination, for our crucial problem has been a lack of conventional means to render our lives believeable. This, my friends, is the crux of solitude."

BACKGROUND

Gabriel García Márquez is often thought of as a writer of fantasy. Critics and reviewers again and again draw attention to the magical qualities of his work. But the underlying structure of García Márquez's "fantasies" follow traditional patterns of storytelling. In "The Handsomest Drowned Man in the World," villagers leading perfectly ordinary lives are changed forever by the appearance of a stranger in their midst. The shape of the story is a familiar one. What is unfamiliar or magical is that the stranger turned out to be a stunningly handsome dead man. As the villagers create a mythology for Esteban out of their own imaginations, they are in fact recreating themselves and the story of their village.

FOR DISCUSSION AND REFLECTION

➤ Do you think that the townspeople's creation of a story for the handsome drowned man is a criticism of their simple ways or a commentary on man's need to create myths? (Both views are defensible.)

➤ What are Esteban's legendary qualities? (his size, his strength, his power to focus attention on himself even after death)

➤ What human details about Esteban might also be immortalized in legend? (his embarrassment at breaking chairs, cracking his head on crossbeams, knowing how others saw him)

Writing

QUICK ASSESS

Do students' lyrics:

✓ demonstrate an understanding of Esteban's legendary qualities?

✓ use details from the story?

✓ embroider upon the truth of what happened?

As students prepare to recast the story of Esteban into song, help them think about how the events of that day when the body washed up onto shore might be retold years later. What details are likely to change? Which are likely to remain the same? Have the students think of songs they know which celebrate particular individuals.

READING AND WRITING EXTENSIONS

➤ Read aloud "Light Is Like Water," a García Márquez short story from his collection *Strange Pilgrims*. In this story the scientific realities of light and water are turned on their head when the narrator (who seems to resemble the author) is asked by a young boy why the light went on with just the touch of a switch. The narrator replies, "Light is like water. You turn the tap and out it comes." The result of this curious response is that, in the story, light begins to behave like water.

➤ Ask students to write a poem called "Light Is Like _____," filling in the blank with other words to describe light's extraordinary qualities.

Three Reinterpretations

Critical Reading

FOCUS

Sometimes writers make us see a traditional story in a different way.

BACKGROUND

"Lot's Wife," by Anna Akhmatova, is a retelling of the story from Genesis of the destruction of Sodom and Gomorrah. Akhmatova does this from the point of view of Lot's wife, who was turned into a pillar of salt for looking back at what she had left behind.

➤ Many readers are familiar with stories from the Bible: The Garden of Eden, Cain and Abel, Noah's Ark, Job's Trials, Abraham and Isaac. Knowing this, writers often use characters and events from these familiar stories to tell their own. In so doing, they create an entirely new work of art and also often cause active readers to think about the old story in new ways.

➤ In "Lot's Wife," for example, the poet has shifted the point of view in order to make readers feel compassion for Lot's wife. Reading the Bible story, a reader sees Lot's wife as someone who has disobeyed God and is therefore justly punished. Reading Anna Akhmatova, a reader sees her as a bewildered woman forced to leave everything she has loved and punished for taking one last look.

FOR DISCUSSION AND REFLECTION

➤ In the third line of the poem, "uneasiness" is personified. Ask students to explain the significance of what was said to Lot's wife. ("Uneasiness" tricked Lot's wife into thinking that it wasn't too late to look back.)

➤ Why should Lot's wife be uneasy? (She is walking away from the world she knows, much that she has loved.)

➤ Why does the speaker say that she will never forget Lot's wife, "She who gave up her life to steal one glance"? (In this odd footnote to the story of Sodom and Gomorrah's destruction, the poet has recognized the story of a brave and suffering woman.)

Writing

QUICK ASSESS

Do students' paragraphs :

✓ explain what the poet has added of her own to the story?

✓ describe specific references that Akhmatova makes to the Genesis story?

Create a chart on the board where students can list the similarities and differences in these two versions of a story. This will help students to explain Akhmatova's interpretation of the Bible story with greater specificity.

READING AND WRITING EXTENSIONS

➤ Choose another familiar story from the Old Testament—Adam and Eve, the Tower of Babel, Noah's Ark, Jonah and the Whale—and retell this story in the form of a poem. Allow students to focus on one small detail of the story the way Akhmatova has done, if they wish.

➤ Have students find another poem which retells a familiar story. Hold a class discussion on the different ways poets retell the stories. Are there common elements among their methods?

Four Timeless Stories

Critical Reading

FOCUS

Timeless stories speak to us across years and miles.

BACKGROUND

Anna Akhmatova was born in 1889 in Odessa. She married in 1910 to a poet, Nikolai Gumilev, and published her own first collection of poems in 1912. With this early book, she became one of the bright young talents of the Russian cultural scene, which included Mendelstam, Prokofiev, Diaghilev, and Stravinsky.

Akhmatova's husband was killed by Bolsheviks as a counter-revolutionary, and she was tainted by association. She lived through the darkest years of Stalinist terror. Her son, Lev Gumilev, was arrested and sent to labor camps, as was Akhmatova's companion in her later years, Nikolai Punin, an art critic. Her major works *Requiem* and *Poem without a Hero* are inspired in large part by these arrests of her loved ones.

Akhmatova herself suffered a kind of exile too. She was expelled from the Writer's Union and not officially accepted by the state. As a result, she worked without assurance her poems would ever reach a wider audience.

FOR DISCUSSION AND REFLECTION

➤ What would motivate a writer to retell a story? (Possible responses include disagreement with the traditional story or the viewpoint from which it was told, a fondness for the story, a new analysis of the story's moral.)

➤ Why would a poet choose to use a Bible story to talk about a contemporary experience? (By borrowing the outline of a powerful story, one that is part of a reader's cultural heritage, a writer accomplishes both a re-examination of the old story and a fashioning of the new within a familiar structure.)

Writing

QUICK ASSESS

Do students' responses:

✓ draw connections between Lot's story and their own lives?

✓ explain particular issues in Lot's story that they find compelling?

In order to help students connect the story of Lot's wife to their own experience, ask them to consider occasions when they have been punished for looking back at what has been rather than staying focused on what lies ahead. Can they remember having "uneasiness shadow" them? What form did the punishment of the gods take for them?

READING AND WRITING EXTENSIONS

➤ Ask students to think about a time when they have tried very hard to achieve a difficult goal but failed. Now tell them the story of Icarus and invite students to retell their story within the framework of this boy who, flying too close to the sun, fell into the sea.

➤ Read W. H. Auden's poem "Musée des Beaux Arts." Ask students to discuss how the poet has used the Icarus myth in a twentieth century retelling of an ancient story.

Five Changing Perspectives

Critical Reading

FOCUS

From *The History of Jack and the Beanstalk*, published in 1820:

"In days of yore, there lived a widow who had a son named Jack. Being an only child, he was too much indulged, and became so extravagant and careless, that he wasted the property which his mother possessed, until at last there remained only a cow, the chief support of her and her son."

BACKGROUND

If the class's combined knowledge of "Jack and the Beanstalk" is missing pieces, bring in a library copy of the fairy tale or type "Jack" and "Beanstalk" into any search engine for the Internet. Important events in the story include these: Jack trades his mother's cow for a handful of beans; the magical beans grow into a huge beanstalk stretching up to the house of a giant (in more detailed versions of the story this giant had long ago killed Jack's father and stolen his gold); Jack climbs the beanstalk three times, each time persuading the giant's wife to hide him; Jack steals the giant's stolen treasures—the goose that laid the golden eggs, a singing harp, and bags of gold; the giant chases Jack down the beanstalk; Jack chops down the overgrown plant causing the giant to crash to earth and die; Jack keeps the gold.

FOR DISCUSSION AND REFLECTION

➤ What lines in the poem offer evidence that it is being told long after Jack's adventures with the beanstalk? ("And the year sinking in its journey," "Now, the oven's stiff creaking / Vexes you," "rustling, your daughter's yellow hair," "Sometimes, in your good memory")

➤ How would you characterize the tone of this poem? Is Jack enjoying a comfortable life at home or is he longing for the good old days? (The tone is somber, regretful, resentful of what is gone forever: "You know then you can never regain / The land that the harp sang so loudly.")

Writing

QUICK ASSESS

Do students' stories:

✔ demonstrate how shifting the point of view from which a story is told changes the nature of the story?

✔ use details from the original story?

✔ help them to see the original story from a new perspective?

Together, brainstorm possible alternative points of view from which the story of "Jack and the Beanstalk" might be told: Jack's poor mother despairing of her son's foolishness, the giant who wants only a nice dinner of human flesh and keeps being annoyed by Jack, the giant's long-suffering wife, or the golden goose.

READING AND WRITING EXTENSIONS

➤ Alfred Lord Tennyson wrote his famous poem "Ulysses" from the point of view of an aging Odysseus: "It little profits that an idle king, / By this still hearth, among these barren crags, / Match'd with an aged wife, I mete and dole / Unequal laws to a savage race." Tennyson imagines that the hero has grown tired of his quiet, peaceful life on Ithaca and once again longs to voyage out on the sea for adventure. Read Tennyson's poem to students and ask them to compare it with Randall Jarrell's "Jack."

➤ Ask students to think of another young, active hero from literature or the movies and then imagine this hero in old age (Superman, Indiana Jones, Tom Sawyer, Holden Caulfield). Have students write a diary entry this hero might make on his eightieth birthday.

ASKING QUESTIONS ABOUT POEMS

Unit Overview

In this unit students will explore an important strategy for understanding poetry: asking questions about what they read. By analyzing a variety of poems, students will learn to develop different kinds of questions and, as a result, sharpen and deepen their interpretive skills.

Literature Focus

	Lesson	Literature
1.	Literal Understanding	**James Wright,** "A Blessing" (Poetry)
2.	Layers of Meaning	**Naoshi Koriyama,** "Unfolding Bud" (Poetry)
3.	Asking Interpretive Questions	**Nina Cassian,** "A Man" (Poetry)
4.	Language and Structure	**David Wagoner,** "Every Good Boy Does Fine" (Poetry)
5.	Speculative Questions	

Reading Focus

1. Asking questions about the speaker, the situation, and the subject of a poem will help you understand its literal meaning.
2. Asking questions about the comparisons a writer makes is a good way to discover layers of meaning.
3. A series of effective questions can help you at each step of interpreting a poem.
4. Studying language and structure will help you interpret a poem.
5. Generating alternatives for elements of a poem can improve your understanding and interpretation.

Writing Focus

1. Write two or three questions you could ask about a poem.
2. Explain the literal meaning and then the second layer of meaning of a poem.
3. Write a brief interpretation.
4. Collect information and answer questions about a poem's structure and language.
5. Write a new poem based on a speculation about another poem.

One Literal Understanding

Critical Reading

FOCUS

Before a reader can approach a poem's metaphorical meaning, it is essential to understand its literal meaning.

BACKGROUND

Before students can begin to analyze a poem, they need to understand it on a literal level. One way to check is to have students explain the who, what, where, when, and why of a poem. Unlike a news story, not every poem will carry all this information, but simply posing the questions pushes students to identify who the speaker is or seems to be, what he or she is saying, and where in time and place the actions of the poem are taking place. Most often answering "why" initiates the interpretive process.

➤ In "A Blessing," by James Wright, the narrator and his friend enter a pasture where two Indian ponies have been grazing. The horses seem to be delighted at the prospect of company and welcome their visitors warmly. The black and white female approaches the narrator and nuzzles his hand. He in turn caresses her long ear which is "delicate as the skin over a girl's wrist." It is a moment of joy.

➤ James Wright won the Pulitzer Prize for Poetry in 1972 for his *Collected Poems.*

FOR DISCUSSION AND REFLECTION

➤ How do you know that the horses are pleased by the appearance of the men? ("They ripple tensely, they can hardly contain their happiness / That we have come. / They bow shyly as wet swans.")

➤ What is a "blessing"? (Most commonly used to mean a short prayer, a blessing also refers to something one is glad of.)

➤ Why do you think James Wright used this word for the title of his poem? (For the narrator this meeting with the Indian ponies has been an unsought and joyous gift.)

➤ What evidence can you find in the poem that supports the view that it is the unexpected meeting between man and horse that is the blessing referred to in the title? ("Suddenly I realize / That if I stepped out of my body I would break / Into blossom.")

Writing

QUICK ASSESS

Do students' charts:

✓ contain thoughtful questions about the poem's speaker, situation, and subject?

✓ answer the questions with quotations from the poem?

In order to assist students as they formulate questions for their chart, put the words *who, what, where, when, why,* and *how* up on the blackboard. Let them know that there may be some questions they pose for which the poem may not be able to provide answers.

READING AND WRITING EXTENSIONS

➤ Invite students to write a short story or poem about an interaction they have had with an animal. Remind them to include information about who, what, where, when, why, and how in their piece of writing.

➤ Ask students to imagine a conversation they would like to have with James Wright. Have them write 2-3 questions about the poem they would like answered.

Two Layers of Meaning

Critical Reading

FOCUS

With thoughtful rereading, a poem will open up like a water-lily bud. Poetry unfolds to reveal a rich inner self.

BACKGROUND

In "Unfolding Bud," by Naoshi Koriyama, the writer compares a poem to a water-lily bud. Ask if anyone in the class can describe what a water-lily bud looks like. If no one can, explain or provide a picture. Without this literal information students will be unable to make a meaningful comparison.

➤ Just as a water-lily bud unfolds a bit more each day, becoming richer and fuller, so a poem which is also "tight-closed" unfolds for the careful reader. Rereading a poem, we discover layers of meaning that were hidden to us at first.

➤ Student readers are often frustrated by poetry because it refuses to say what it means directly. Koriyama's comparison of a budded flower to a poem may help some young readers see the beauty in poetry's layers of meaning.

FOR DISCUSSION AND REFLECTION

➤ Why is one "not amazed / At first glance, / By a poem"? (A poem is a slight thing; it uses few words and takes up very little space in the world. A poem is easy to overlook.)

➤ How is a poem "tight-closed / As a tiny bud"? (A poem's "rich inner self" is often hidden under layers of meaning — literal or metaphorical — that need to be understood before the poem will open itself up to the reader.)

Writing

QUICK ASSESS

Do students' paragraphs:

✔ describe a second layer of meaning beyond the literal?

✔ use specific text references to support their interpretations?

As students write about a second layer of meaning in "A Blessing," make sure they use words and lines from Wright's poem to support their interpretation. While rich poems are open to many possible interpretations, they do not mean just anything the reader wants them to mean.

READING AND WRITING EXTENSIONS

➤ Poems, like onions, contain many layers of meaning. To make this comparison concrete for students, bring in a multi-layered vegetable (if you choose a small one like a Brussels sprout, you can give one to each student) and have students imagine that the vegetable represents who they are today, sitting in a desk in class. As they peel it apart, leaf by leaf, have students write about the layers of themselves from the most public to the most private.

➤ Have students bring in a favorite poem of theirs that has unfolded for them over time and share it with their classmates. Bring in one of yours.

Three Asking Interpretive Questions

Critical Reading

FOCUS

Formulating questions helps readers figure out what they need to know in order to make a poem unfold.

BACKGROUND

Interpreting a poem requires that a reader explain the actions, events, or statements in a poem. We accomplish this either by examining inner relationships within the poem or by relating the particulars in the poem to general principles.

➤ In Nina Cassian's poem "A Man," the subject of the poem has lost an arm in a war. At first he is afraid and thinks only of the things he will no longer be able to do: play the piano, hold the woman he loves, applaud with two hands. But instead of giving in to despair, the man determines to use the one arm he has left with twice the energy and heart. The poem is a tribute to the inner resources that give the man (unnamed) the strength to resume his life as before. The wing that grows where, in the service of his country, "the arm had been torn away," represents the man's belief in himself.

FOR DISCUSSION AND REFLECTION

➤ Why do you think the poet has chosen to write the middle lines of her poem as a direct quotation from the man who has lost his arm? (The reader can hear his complaint and feel the loss more acutely than if we were told of it second-hand.)

➤ What is the difference between the man's first analysis of his situation, that he would "only be able to do things by halves" and his final determination? (Instead of feeling only half a man, he sets himself to do "everything with twice as much enthusiasm.")

➤ Explain the metaphor of a wing. (Symbolic of flight and freedom, the wing represents the man's determination to return to normal life.)

Writing

QUICK ASSESS

Do students' interpretive paragraphs:

✓ draw conclusions about the poem that reflect careful reading?

✓ use specific details from the poem to support their conclusions?

Allow students to test their interpretations of the poem with one another before they begin to write. Invite them to challenge one another's interpretations. Defending the inferences they have drawn will help to make their paragraphs stronger.

READING AND WRITING EXTENSIONS

➤ Have students imagine they are the wife of the man in Nina Cassian's poem "A Man." Ask them to write a diary entry for the day when she first hears that her husband has lost his arm in the war. Write a second entry for the day when he discovers that where once there was an arm, a wing had grown.

➤ Invite students to turn Nina Cassian's poem into a story. Before they begin, be sure they decide whether they are going to tell this story from the point of view of the man, his wife, or an omniscient narrator.

Four Language and Structure

Critical Reading

FOCUS

The meaning of the poem is developed through the language and structure a poet chooses.

BACKGROUND

The title of the poem "Every Good Boy Does Fine" works on several levels of meaning. On one level, it reminds readers of the phrase everyone who has taken music lessons learned in order to remember the notes corresponding to the lines of the treble clef. Within the context of the poem, the title has another level of meaning. David Wagoner's speaker describes a series of things that he tried to achieve but failed at miserably. In this respect, every good boy clearly did not do fine. The poem does not end in failure, however, because right before our eyes is evidence that though this good boy never became a great cornet player or a basketball star or a football player, he did all right for himself. Winning "in the long run," he wrote this poem.

➣ A *cornet* is a small brass instrument like a trumpet.

➣ *Coda* refers to the concluding passage of a piece of music.

FOR DISCUSSION AND REFLECTION

➣ What are the three activities that the speaker describes having attempted as a young man? (playing a trumpet, playing basketball, playing football)

➣ What evidence can you find in the poem that demonstrates the speaker was not much good at any of these endeavors? (Nervous in performance, his solo wobbled. Hopelessly forgetful, he left behind his basketball "shoes, socks, uniform." Even when an intercepted football seems sure to bring him heroic status, a safety brings him down.)

➣ Where does the narrator find success? (It's in the poem you have before you.)

Writing

QUICK ASSESS

Do students' charts:

✓ contain thoughtful questions and answers?

✓ reflect understanding of the poem's coda and its resolution for the narrator?

Students are asked to complete a chart about how the meaning of the poem is developed through David Wagoner's choice of language and structure. For some students, the language specific to music may be familiar. Others may recognize the language specific to sports. Invite them to consider how the meaning of a poem can be hidden without knowledge of this vocabulary.

READING AND WRITING EXTENSIONS

➣ Have students recall a time when they felt a hopeless failure at something. Have them describe what happened, in poetry or prose, as David Wagoner has, concluding with a description of something they have discovered that they can do well.

➣ Have students imagine that a tenth grader at their school who is an aspiring actress has just read the posted cast list for the school play. Seeing that her name is nowhere to be found, she angrily marches away, telling everyone to leave her alone. Ask students to imagine they see her and attempt to offer consolation. Have them write the dialogue for this scene.

Five Speculative Questions

Critical Reading

FOCUS

Audre Lorde on poetry:

"Poetry is not a luxury. It is a necessity of our existence. It forms the quality of light within which we predicate our hopes and dreams towards survival and change."

BACKGROUND

When we speculate about a piece of literature, we form an opinion without definite knowledge or evidence. Speculation is both a dangerous and a potentially powerful act for a reader to engage in. Students who are good at coming up with "right answers" may be uncomfortable with the invitation to speculate, but others who have less to lose may find this a useful path to learning how to interpret literature. Asking students to rearrange the pieces of a text and speculate on new meanings allows them enormous interpretive range.

FOR DISCUSSION AND REFLECTION

➤ Brainstorm on the board a series of "What if . . ." sentences. (What if the one-armed man had despaired? What if the Indian ponies had reared up against Wright's narrator? What if the boy in "Every Good Boy Does Fine" had won a prize with his cornet?)

➤ Tobias Wolff has written that, "In the arms of language, children will discover the family of humanity. They will learn what has gone before, and they will learn what is left to be done. In language they will learn to laugh, and to grieve, to be consoled in their grief, and to console others. In language they will discover who they are." Ask students to articulate what they have learned from their reading of "A Blessing," "Unfolding Bud," "A Man," and "Every Good Boy Does Fine." What have these poets taught them about the family of humanity? (Responses will vary.)

Writing

QUICK ASSESS

Do students' poems:

✓ demonstrate a willingness to play with language and literature?

✓ reflect an understanding of the poems they have read?

Students are asked to write a poem of their own based upon one of their speculations. To help them get started, have students share their speculative questions about one of the poems in the unit. The speculation that one student discards may be just the thing another one can use. Encourage them to share.

READING AND WRITING EXTENSIONS

➤ Imagine that the one-armed man (after he had sprouted a wing) met with the narrator of "Every Good Boy Does Fine" soon after he had been brought down by the safety. What advice do students think this veteran would have for the disheartened football player?

➤ Have students imagine they have been asked to make a speech to the Board of Education explaining that "poetry is not a luxury." Ask them to write a speech in which they persuade their listeners to fund the purchase of 100 new books of poetry for the school library.

Unit Overview

In "Text and Subtext," students will discover how developing an awareness of a work's subtext can make them better active readers. As they read and respond to two short stories and a poem, students will learn to fill in background information, recognize irony, evaluate tone and point of view, and challenge the assumptions of the author.

Literature Focus

Lesson	Literature
1. Supplying the Background	**S. I. Kishor,** "Appointment with Love" (Short Story)
2. Shifting Point of View	
3. Understanding Irony	**John Collier,** "The Chaser" (Short Story)
4. Examining Assumptions	
5. Understanding Tone	**Dorothy Parker,** "One Perfect Rose" (Poetry)

Reading Focus

1. Supplying the implied background for characters' actions is an important element of active reading.
2. By shifting the point of view, you can enlarge your interpretation of the story and understanding of human nature.
3. Understanding what is not said is essential to understanding a story, especially one that uses irony.
4. What we understand and enjoy in our reading is often influenced by how much we share the author's assumptions about the subject.
5. Tone is an important aspect of the subtext. To understand it, pay attention to the author's words and what they imply.

Writing Focus

1. Write a diary entry that supplies background information about a character.
2. Rewrite a story by shifting the point of view.
3. Identify and explain examples of verbal irony.
4. Explore how your enjoyment of a story is influenced by whether you share the author's assumptions about the subject.
5. Rewrite a poem by changing the tone.

One Supplying the Background

Critical Reading

FOCUS

The subtext is a collection of meanings implied by the author and supplied by the reader.

BACKGROUND

Reading comprehension is often dependent upon background knowledge. Simply being able to read the words on a page and understand the meaning of those words is not enough. A reader needs to understand the implications of these words.

➤ For example, the story "Appointment with Love," by S. I. Kishor, takes place in Grand Central Station, a particular location in New York City. The words "Grand Central Station" imply a busy, bustling place full of people hurrying to be somewhere else. While standing amidst this crowd the young Army lieutenant remembers "when his plane had been caught in the midst of a pack of Zeros." Most readers would be able to guess that he is returning from a war, but background knowledge about airplanes would provide you with the additional information that this was World War II, and Lieutenant Blandford has been fighting the Japanese. Hollis's inspirational message which refers to King David and the Twenty-third Psalm would resonate for a reader familiar with the Bible.

➤ The novel that triggered the meeting between Lieutenant Blandford and Hollis Meynell was *Of Human Bondage*. Though the author of this story never makes mention of it, readers with a background knowledge of literature would know that this semiautobiographical novel by W. Somerset Maugham depicts a young medical student's painful progress toward maturity and his search for love. A reader who knows this background information about the book Lieutenant Blandford carries has a clue that Kishor's story will end happily.

FOR DISCUSSION AND REFLECTION

➤ Ask students to find places or details in the story that puzzled them. Let them know that this is a common experience for all readers. The good news is that the more we read, the more background knowledge we acquire. (Responses will vary.)

➤ Did you think Hollis was going to be a physically attractive or a homely woman? (Have students point to the evidence in the story that supports their inferences.)

Writing

QUICK ASSESS

Do students' diary entries:

✓ use concrete details from the story?

✓ reflect an understanding of Hollis Meynell's character?

➤ Before students begin to write a diary entry from the point of view of Hollis Meynell, have them make a list on the board of words and phrases from the story that describe her.

READING AND WRITING EXTENSIONS

➤ Though the 40-year-old woman who carries Hollis's flower makes only a cameo appearance in the story, she is powerfully characterized in those few lines. Write an imaginary phone conversation that she might have had that night with a friend describing what happened to her in Grand Central Station.

➤ Ask students to imagine they are making a movie of this story. Whom would they cast as Hollis and as Lieutenant Blandford?

Two Shifting Point of View

Critical Reading

FOCUS
Point of view is the perspective from which a story is presented to the reader.

BACKGROUND

A writer has a number of options when deciding how to present events. One of the most important technical decisions a writer makes is choosing which point of view to use. Point of view is determined by who is telling the story and the degree of knowledge this person possesses. When choosing a point of view for a story, writers must decide how involved they want the reader to be in the thoughts and actions of the characters, how much they want revealed, and what vantage point will allow the strongest climax and the most effective resolution.

➤ In "Appointment with Love," the author uses a first-person point of view. All events are seen through the eyes of Lieutenant Blandford. The reader is only told explicitly what he is thinking and feeling. As a result, neither Blandford nor the reader knows key things at the beginning of the story, such as what Hollis Meynell looks like. As students consider what is not said (as much as what is), encourage them to recognize how they add meaning to the author's words from their experiences, assumptions, and imagination.

FOR DISCUSSION AND REFLECTION

➤ How does not knowing what Hollis looks like build suspense in the story? (The reader experiences Lieutenant Blandford's nervousness and insecurity as he stands waiting next to the information booth in Grand Central Station.)

➤ What can you infer about Hollis Meynell from the story? (She is intelligent, discerning, and judicious. She reads serious fiction, writes wise letters, and is cautious about the way people view her.)

➤ What might Hollis Meynell be doing and thinking as she waits in the restaurant? (Responses will vary.)

Writing

QUICK ASSESS
Do students' stories:

✓ use concrete details from the original story when they retell it?

✓ shift the point of view of the story from Blandford's to Hollis Meynell's?

Students are asked to rewrite the story from the point of view of Hollis Meynell. Begin by asking them if they think that the title, "Appointment with Love," should remain the same or change. Encourage them to share their stories with classmates and note similarities and differences in the different versions.

READING AND WRITING EXTENSIONS

➤ In William Butler Yeats's poem "For Anne Gregory," a man and a young woman debate the question of whether or not anyone could "Love you for yourself alone / And not your yellow hair." The girl insists that she could dye it brown or black and then she could be loved for herself. His response is that "only God, my dear, / Could love you for yourself alone / And not your yellow hair." Ask students to compare this young woman's dilemma with Hollis Meynell's.

➤ Have students write about a time when they feel they were judged unfairly on the basis of how they looked (too short to be a good basketball player, too pretty to be smart, too young to be taken seriously).

Three **Understanding Irony**

Critical Reading

FOCUS
Verbal irony is the difference between what a speaker says and what he or she means.

BACKGROUND
Irony produces a wry, humorous effect by bringing in a part of the truth that we might have preferred to hide. It often has the last word, undercutting the more flattering or idealizing hypothesis.

➤ In "The Chaser," there is a sad and comic contrast between expectation and event, between ideal and reality. Alan Austen is in love with a woman who does not love him. He expects to solve this problem with a magic potion. The old man who furnishes him with the mixture knows the reality of what is likely to happen next. The kind of love that the potion synthetically creates will over time become suffocating to Austen and cause him to need another kind of chemical solution.

➤ By the end of "The Chaser," the alert reader experiences the special irony of knowing more than the naive Austen. Like the old man, we are fairly certain that he will be back one day for the very expensive "glove-cleaner."

FOR DISCUSSION AND REFLECTION
➤ What evidence do you have that Alan Austen is an inexperienced young man? (He arrives "nervous as a kitten." He speaks hesitantly and with many pauses.)

➤ What evidence can you find that he is also a foolish young man? (He wants to be his lover's "sole interest in life." He cannot hear the old man's warning in the story about the "glove-cleaner" potion.)

➤ Explain the irony inherent in the old man's comment, "Young people who need a love potion very seldom have five thousand dollars. Otherwise they would not need a love potion." (Given human folly, in most circumstances money is itself a powerful love potion.)

Writing

QUICK ASSESS
Do students' charts:

✓ identify examples of verbal irony in the story?

✓ explain how these examples often express a meaning that is opposite of their literal meaning?

As students collect examples of verbal irony from the story, allow them to explain what they have found to one another before they fill in the second column. It is difficult to describe succinctly what is ironic about an expression.

READING AND WRITING EXTENSIONS
On page 22, students read the story of King Midas. As in John Collier's story "The Chaser," the main character received something that he believed would be of great benefit to him. For Alan Austen it was a love potion, for King Midas the touch of gold. Have students reread the myth and compare what happens to King Midas with what the old man in "The Chaser" believes will happen to Alan Austen. (The things we unwisely covet—gold, the obsessive love of a woman—can be our undoing.)

➤ Ask students to write about a time when they coveted and then owned something that turned out to be bad for them over time (a phone of their own, a television in their room, a pager).

Four Examining Assumptions

Critical Reading

FOCUS

Active readers challenge the assumptions an author makes in fiction.

BACKGROUND

When a reader or a writer "assumes" something, he or she takes the position that something is true or sure to happen before there is proof. Often there can be a discrepancy between what a writer assumes to be true and what the reader assumes.

➤ The authors of "Appointment with Love" and "The Chaser" make assumptions about the nature of love and male-female relationships that may or may not correspond with students' assumptions. Kishor assumes that for love to flourish between Lieutenant Blandford and Hollis Meynell that she cannot look like the dumpy woman carrying the flower. Collier assumes that obsessive love will, over time, turn to loathing.

FOR DISCUSSION AND REFLECTION

Ask students to picture in their mind's eye the ideal couple and then answer the following questions:

➤ Is the man older than the woman?

➤ Is he bigger than the woman?

➤ Is he smarter or better educated than the woman?

➤ Does he have a better-paying job than the woman?

➤ Are the man and woman jealous of each other?

➤ Does each have other friends of the opposite sex?

➤ Is she beautiful? Is he handsome? Is this important?

➤ Based upon their reading of these two stories, how do students think S. I. Kishor and John Collier would answer these questions? (Responses will vary.)

Writing

QUICK ASSESS

Do students' paragraphs:

✔ identify the assumptions each author has made?

✔ explain their preferences based upon their reactions to the authors' assumptions?

Students are asked to write a paragraph in which they tell whether they preferred S. I. Kishor's "Appointment with Love" or John Collier's "The Chaser." In order to clarify their opinions, it may help to ask students to identify specific places in the stories where the assumptions the writers made were different from their own assumptions about male-female relationships.

READING AND WRITING EXTENSIONS

➤ Have students imagine they are Diana from John Collier's story "The Chaser." Write two entries in her diary, one for the day before Alan visits the old man, another for the day after Alan has slipped the magic potion into her glass of wine.

➤ Ask students to write a Valentine note to their imaginary ideal love. Be sure to include in the poem details that indicate what it is about this person that makes him or her ideal.

Five Understanding Tone

Critical Reading

FOCUS

Sven Birkerts on tone:

"The tone of a work might be defined as *how* the *what* gets told."

BACKGROUND

Tone is directly related to point of view. How the story is told depends on who is telling it and has everything to do with the narrator's relation to the events.

➤ In "One Perfect Rose," Dorothy Parker describes her response to a gift from a lover. In the first two stanzas the reader is lulled into believing (that is, unless the reader is familiar with Dorothy Parker) that the narrator is pleased with the flower. In the final stanza the poem takes an ironic turn. With the line "Why is it no one ever sent me yet / One perfect limousine," the reader is forced to reassess Parker's attitude towards this "one perfect rose."

➤ Parker is a master of irony. In her book review column for *Vanity Fair* she wrote, "This is not a novel to be tossed aside lightly. It should be thrown with great force." The irony of this statement is that we expect the cliché of her first sentence to be followed by praise. Instead Parker proceeds to attack the book.

FOR DISCUSSION AND REFLECTION

➤ What word in the poem is the first clue to the shift in tone from romantic to cynical? (limousine)

➤ What are the connotations of the word "limousine" that cause the reader to revise his or her opinion of the narrator? (Instead of assuming she is a sentimental romantic gushing over a flower, the reader is faced with the narrator's caustic rejection of romantic sentiment.)

➤ Ask students to review the definition of irony (the contrast between expectation and reality) and to explain how Dorothy Parker makes use of irony in this poem. (We expect the narrator to behave as most lovers would and be thrilled to receive one perfect rose. Instead she complains.)

Writing

QUICK ASSESS

Do students' poems:

✔ recast the poem in a different tone?

✔ reflect a thoughtful choice of words?

Help students recognize the two different tones in Parker's poem as they begin choosing a tone for their own poems. Have them identify the kind of word choices that will contribute to this tone and communicate their attitude toward the gift of a rose.

READING AND WRITING EXTENSIONS

➤ Dorothy Parker examined the social mores of her day with biting wit and perceptive insight. Her own life exemplified this duality, for while she was one of the most talked-about women of her day, rich and gifted, she was also known as "a masochist whose passion for unhappiness knew no bounds." Ask students to write about how a preference for one perfect limousine over one perfect rose could be a recipe for unhappiness in love.

➤ Read other poems of Dorothy Parker's to students and have a discussion about their tone. Does there seem to be a consistency in *how* the *what* gets told?

Unit Overview

In "Poetry and Craft," students will explore how form affects our reading of a poem. As they read light verse by Ogden Nash and sonnets by William Meredith, William Shakespeare, Edna St. Vincent Millay, and Barbara Greenberg, students will learn about rhyme scheme, meter, stanza pattern, limericks, and both Italian and Shakespearean sonnets.

Literature Focus

	Lesson	Literature
1.	Light Verse	**Ogden Nash,** "The trouble with a kitten" (Poetry) Limericks (Poetry)
2.	Reading a Poem for Meaning	**William Meredith,** "The Illiterate" (Poetry)
3.	The Italian Sonnet	
4.	The Shakespearean Sonnet	**William Shakespeare,** Sonnet 116 "Let me not to the marriage of true minds" (Poetry) **Edna St. Vincent Millay,** "Pity Me Not" (Poetry)
5.	The Modern Sonnet	**Barbara Greenberg,** "I Really Do Live by the Sea" (Poetry)

Reading Focus

1. Light verse makes use of rhyme and rhythm in a playful, humorous, even nonsensical way.

2. The first step in reading a poem is to look carefully at what the poet is saying. You may be aware of the form, but don't focus on it until you understand the meaning.

3. The sonnet is a fourteen-line poem which establishes a situation and then comments on it.

4. The organization of the Shakespearean sonnet provides a basis for posing a question or idea and then providing a resolution in the final two lines.

5. Exploring your own ideas about form in poetry will help you become a more observant reader of poetry. It will also give you ideas about how to shape poems you might like to write yourself.

Writing Focus

1. Write a limerick, following established patterns of rhyme and rhythm.

2. Write down ideas and questions about the meaning of a poem's title.

3. Write a paragraph about form and meaning in an Italian sonnet.

4. Analyze the organization of a Shakespearean sonnet.

5. Describe your views about form in poetry, using several poems as examples.

One Light Verse

C r i t i c a l R e a d i n g

BACKGROUND

Light verse makes stringent demands on the writer's technique. A fault in scansion or rhyme, an awkwardness or obscurity can ruin the whole poem. Light verse is *light*, light in the sense of cheerful, airy, light as in light-footed and light-hearted, "requiring little mental effort, amusing, entertaining." *(Oxford English Dictionary)*

➤ According to A. A. Milne, "Light verse obeys Coleridge's definition of poetry, the best words in the best order; it demands Carlyle's definition of Genius, transcendent capacity for taking pains; and it is the supreme exhibition of somebody's definition of art, the concealment of art. In the result it observes the most exact laws of rhythm and meter as if by a happy accident, and in a sort of nonchalant spirit of mockery at the real poets who do it on purpose." *(Year In, Year Out, 1952)*

FOR DISCUSSION AND REFLECTION

➤ What effect does the rhythm of a limerick have on you as a reader? (Regular meter adds emphasis. It also makes a poem easier to remember.)

➤ What effect does the rhyme at the end of a line have on you as a reader? (It brings a sense of order and inevitability to a poem as well as, in the case of limericks, levity or even absurdity. Rhyme also facilitates memorization.)

➤ Ask students why they think the limerick is such a popular form. (Responses will vary.)

W r i t i n g

QUICK ASSESS

Do students' limericks:

✓ follow the established rhyme pattern?

✓ follow the established rhythm pattern?

In order to check the rhyme scheme and rhythm pattern of their limericks, have students read them aloud. Discrepancies in meter can be heard immediately. Make available a rhyming dictionary from your school library to help students avoid clichéd rhymes.

READING AND WRITING EXTENSIONS

➤ Limericks are often ribald, but a good source of limericks suitable for classroom use is Edward Lear's *Book of Nonsense* (1846). He claimed to have gotten the idea from a nursery rhyme beginning "There was an old man of Tobago." Many, like this one, have only Anonymous listed as their author:

> An oyster from Kalamazoo
> Confessed he was feeling quite blue,
>   "For," he said, "as a rule,
>   When the weather turns cool,
> I invariably get in a stew!"

Working with partners, have students compose another limerick that begins, "A(n) _____ from _____ ." Insert a place name from a familiar city or town in the second blank.

➤ Have students write a short reflective essay entitled "In Praise of Light Verse."

Two Reading a Poem for Meaning

Critical Reading

FOCUS

The meaning of the poem may not be obvious.

BACKGROUND

"The Illiterate" by William Meredith begins with a simile. The poet describes the experience of "Touching your goodness" by comparing it with the experience of an illiterate man touching a letter. Before students can explore this comparison, they will need to figure out exactly what Meredith is saying it would be like to receive a letter possibly bearing news of enormous importance and be unable to read it for oneself. He imagines the possibilities: his uncle leaving him the farm, his parents dying, the woman he loves deciding that she returns his affection. His solution, "Afraid and letter-proud," is to keep the letter with him, unread.

FOR DISCUSSION AND REFLECTION

➤ Ask students what they make of the rhyme scheme in "The Illiterate." (The poet uses the repetition of whole words to end lines rather than rhyming words. A word does, however, rhyme with itself.)

➤ How does this unusual word choice affect your reading of the poem? (It lends a spareness to the work as though the writer is being careful not to spend too many words.)

➤ Why is this man "afraid"? (He fears what news, good or bad, that he might have in his hand unopened.)

➤ Why is this man "ashamed"? (He cannot read.)

➤ What might William Meredith be saying about the experience of "Touching your goodness" when he compares it with the illiterate man turning "a letter over in his hand"? (By drawing a parallel between the narrator and the illiterate, the poet suggests that just as the words on a page are indecipherable to someone who cannot read, so is the goodness embodied by the person addressed unfathomable. Like the illiterate man, the narrator wants to keep this goodness close to him, all the while knowing that he will never understand it. Also like the illiterate man, he is too proud to ask for help from anyone else.)

Writing

QUICK ASSESS

Do students' responses:

✓ demonstrate understanding of Meredith's poem?

✓ focus on the title's meaning?

As students formulate their ideas about the meaning of the title, have them think about the connotations of "illiterate." How does that term set one apart?

READING AND WRITING EXTENSIONS

➤ Invite students to write a poem about something that they know they will never understand. They might choose to use an extended simile as Meredith has.

➤ What would be the worst thing about not being able to read? Have students write informally on this question and then share what they have written with one another. Ask students to remember what it was like before they themselves learned to read.

Three The Italian Sonnet

Critical Reading

FOCUS

From *Poetic Meter and Poetic Form* by Paul Fussell:

"The poet who understands the sonnet form is the one who has developed an instinct for exploiting the principle of imbalance."

BACKGROUND

Everyone knows that poetic meter tends to produce a pleasant effect, but metrical theorists disagree vigorously about the reason for the universal popularity of metered compositions. One argument often advanced to explain the popularity of the sonnet as a poetic form is that our ideas tend to come in units and that the closest approximation to an idea-unit is the fourteen-line sonnet. Needless to say, this cannot be proven.

➤ Petrarchan sonnets like William Meredith's "The Illiterate" have a characteristic turn at the start of line nine. The reader is presented with a logical or emotional shift which allows the speaker to take a new or enlarged view of his subject. In "The Illiterate," the speaker begins to speculate in lines nine through eleven upon the news that the letter he is unable to open might contain. The question asked in the final couplet reminds the reader of the "you" the poem addresses and completes the poet's comparison of the indecipherable letter with the concept of goodness.

FOR DISCUSSION AND REFLECTION

➤ How do the first eight lines describe a problem? (An illiterate man has just received a letter. He is fearful of the news it may contain but embarrassed to ask for help and admit his disability.)

➤ What happens in the space between lines eight and nine? (The man starts to imagine what he cannot decipher. The "problem" becomes more complicated.)

➤ How do these two parts of the sonnet affect you as a reader? (The imbalance between them creates tension. The release of this tension occurs in the closing couplet where the man makes his peace with these words that he will never read.)

Writing

QUICK ASSESS

Do students' responses:

✓ connect the poem's form to its meaning?

✓ interpret the poem's title?

Students are asked to think about how the form of the poem is related to its meaning and to write about how this affects their interpretation of the poem's title. Have them consider whether illiteracy suggests more than simply the inability to read.

READING AND WRITING EXTENSIONS

➤ Have students write the unread letter. Compare these imaginary letters, and ask students to offer evidence from the poem to support their decision concerning the letter's contents.

➤ One of the best-known Petrarchan sonnets in English is "On First Looking into Chapman's Homer," by John Keats. Read this poem and ask students to explain the turn that the poem takes in line nine.

Four The Shakespearean Sonnet

Critical Reading

FOCUS

The final couplet of a Shakespearan sonnet provides a conclusion or resolution:

"If this be error and upon me proved, / I never writ, nor no man ever loved."

BACKGROUND

Although the basic form of both Petrarchan and Shakespearean sonnets is similar, the balance between the "problem" and the "solution" is quite different. The last six lines of a Petrarchan sonnet allow for the problem to be solved in a relatively expansive or meditative process, while the final couplet of a Shakespearean sonnet causes the solution to be most often a paradox or quick bit of wit. This tends to make the Shakespearean sonnet a showpiece of logic or mock-logic.

➤ In Sonnet 116, Shakespeare defines love as steadfast, unshakable, focused, unchangeable. His couplet implies that if the reader can prove this to be untrue, then not only has Shakespeare "never writ" but "no man ever loved."

➤ Edna St. Vincent Millay uses a Shakespearean sonnet to explore a common problem faced by a person in love — though the speaker knows and fully recognizes intellectually that her love is no longer returned, the emotional connection remains intact. Millay says not to pity her that the love has ended but that her heart is so slow to learn what her head knows well.

FOR DISCUSSION AND REFLECTION

➤ Why might a poet choose this most rigorous of poetic forms to write about a subject as loosely defined as "love"? (The form offers the poet a structure around which he or she can construct his or her emerging understanding of what it means "to love.")

➤ How does the repetition of the line "Pity me not" affect you as a reader? (By instructing the listener about what the speaker does not want to be pitied for, she sets us up for what she does lament. It also prepares us for the final couplet's distinction between head and heart.)

➤ Whose definition of love comes closest to your own? (Responses will vary.)

Writing

QUICK ASSESS

Do students' analyses:

✓ explain the points of Millay's argument?

✓ comment on the ideas about love that both poems develop?

Students are instructed to interpret "Pity Me Not" by analyzing the way Millay's thought pattern progresses through the three quatrains and the couplet. Encourage them to make connections between the two sonnets' ideas of love as they write.

READING AND WRITING EXTENSIONS

➤ Create a class collection of favorite love poems. Compile these in a volume of love poetry or post them on a bulletin board. Ask students to think about what these "favorite" poems seem to have in common.

➤ Imagine that Edna St. Vincent Millay has written this poem in response to a letter from the man she loves deeply. Ask students to write what they think might have been his message to her.

Five The Modern Sonnet

Critical Reading

FOCUS

Even if we're not conscious of it, the form of a poem affects our understanding of its meaning.

BACKGROUND

One reason the sonnet form has proven useful is that it is effective for certain types of subject matter, particularly for the serious treatment of love. Barbara Greenberg's variations on the sonnet's form mirror her speaker's state of mind. The poem is not an orderly argument presented in an elegant and logical manner like Shakespeare's and Edna St. Vincent Millay's sonnets. Instead, the speaker seems to juggle with her subject, trying too hard to convince her listener that she really is fine, really. Reaching her final line and the assertion that "I really am happy," the reader infers the exact opposite.

FOR DISCUSSION AND REFLECTION

➤ Why does the speaker repeat that "I really do live by the sea"? (Of all the assertions made, only this one is likely to be true. She attempts to use this geographical fact as a pole against which the other statements should be measured.)

➤ Is the speaker in this poem a reliable narrator? (No. We see what the narrator denies — that she is very unhappy.)

Writing

QUICK ASSESS

Do students' responses:

✓ construct a defensible thesis about form?

✓ use supporting evidence from the poems to develop the thesis?

Reread all of the sonnets aloud as students write about the idea that form allows a poet freedom which complete absence of rules does not.

READING AND WRITING EXTENSIONS

➤ These fourteen lines from Act I, Scene 5 of *Romeo and Juliet* can be read as a sonnet:

Romeo. If I profane with my unworthiest hand
This holy shrine, the gentle sin is this;
My lips, two blushing pilgrims, ready stand
To smooth that rough touch with a tender kiss.
Juliet. Good pilgrim, you do wrong your hand too much,
Which mannerly devotion shows in this;
For saints have hands that pilgrims' hands do touch,
And palm to palm is holy palmers' kiss.
Romeo. Have not saints lips, and holy palmers too?
Juliet. Ay, pilgrim, lips that they must use in prayer.
Romeo. O! then, dear saint, let lips do what hands do;
They pray, Grant thou, lest faith turn to despair.
Juliet. Saints do not move, though grant for prayers' sake.
Romeo. Then move not, while my prayers' effect I take.

Ask whether students think it was intentional that these lines adhere to the meter and rhyme scheme of a sonnet.

➤ Have students write stage directions for these fourteen lines for Romeo and Juliet.

WRITING FROM MODELS: TONE

Unit Overview

In "Writing from Models: Tone," students will learn the value of looking carefully at the tone of a piece of writing. To help them explore how writers use persona, scenarios, diction, and metaphors to convey tone, students will read poetry and nonfiction and practice techniques of modeling.

Literature Focus

	Lesson	Literature
1.	Reading for Tone	**W. H. Auden,** "The Unknown Citizen" (Poetry)
2.	Understanding Tone	**Lyn Lifshin,** "You Understand the Requirements" (Poetry)
3.	Comparing Poems	
4.	Using Metaphors	**Alan Lightman,** from *Einstein's Dreams* (Nonfiction)
5.	The Paralog	

Reading Focus

1. Good readers are alert to the tone of voice in a poem. They read between the lines for meaning.

2. Understanding tone requires close attention to the situation or scenario the writer establishes.

3. Writers often set up the tone of a poem by establishing a scenario and adopting a persona. Sentence patterns and word choices are consistent with the established character.

4. Writers often use metaphors to explain complex ideas or concepts that are difficult to explain.

5. Writing a paralog lets you enter into a dialogue with an author. In this way you can expand your understanding of how writers create tone and mood.

Writing Focus

1. Extend the author's poem by writing additional lines that maintain the tone of the original.

2. Write a short letter about an imagined situation.

3. Compare how two poets use situation, persona, and diction to convey tone.

4. Identify passages with particularly vivid images and explain the reasons for your choices.

5. Write a paralog, paying special attention to consistency of tone.

One Reading for Tone

Critical Reading

FOCUS

From *Sound and Sense* by Laurence Perrine:

"Tone may be defined as the writer's or speaker's attitude toward his subject, his audience, or himself."

BACKGROUND

On a literal level "The Unknown Citizen," by W. H. Auden, is an obituary for JS/07/M/378 in which the man's accomplishments are described in bureaucratic detail. The tone of the poem, however, suggests that it be read on another level. Auden uses the life of this "unknown citizen" to critique and satirize the social organization of his times. Early in the poem the reader is told that in "everything he did he served the Greater Community." He "never got fired," "wasn't a scab or odd in his views," and "held the proper opinions for the time of year." Everything about the man conformed with the status quo and fell within the band of normal behavior, normal in terms of the Greater Community, that is.

➤ Students may need help with the meanings and connotations for *scab* (someone who crosses a strikers' picket line) and *Eugenist* (a person involved in the "improvement" of the human species through genetic engineering).

FOR DISCUSSION AND REFLECTION

➤ Make a list on the board of everything students can tell about the unknown citizen's life. A great deal can be found. Push students to mine the poem for details.

➤ Now ask students what they don't know about this man. (Possible responses include how he felt about his life, whom he loved, what he cared about, what gave him joy, the things that made him sad. Everything personal or individual is left out.)

➤ How does what is missing in the obituary provide a clue to Auden's attitude toward his subject? (All the facts of a man's life added up still cannot provide an answer to the question "Who was he?")

➤ Explain the irony and allusion in the poem's title. (Typically, monuments are erected in memory of unknown soldiers, men who have served their country valiantly but died unidentified. The functionary of the state who wrote this obituary for the unknown citizen had a great deal of information about the man, yet he remains "unknown.")

Writing

QUICK ASSESS

Do students' additions:

✓ enhance the poem's meaning?

✓ reproduce the poet's tone?

Students are asked to insert into Auden's poem lines of their own describing additional ways the unknown citizen served the Greater Community. To help them get started, model on the board sample lines that maintain Auden's tone.

READING AND WRITING EXTENSIONS

➤ The details of "The Unknown Citizen" in some ways date it. Auden was critiquing life in Britain after World War II. Have students write an updated version of this obituary for an unknown citizen who sat in front of a computer screen eight hours a day and bought all the technological gadgets of our times.

➤ The inscription on the Tomb of the Unknowns in Arlington National Cemetery in Virginia reads: "Here rests in honored glory an American soldier known but to God." Ask students to analyze the tone of this inscription.

Two Understanding Tone

Critical Reading

FOCUS

Critical readers pay attention to the tone of voice in a poem:

"final regret your disappointment / the unsuccessfully completed best / wishes for the future / it has been a / regret sorry the requirements / the university policy / please don't call us."

BACKGROUND

Tone is the emotional coloring of a poem. Until we can make sense of its tone, a poem is often indecipherable. In "You Understand the Requirements," Lyn Lifshin reproduces the emotional experience of reading a rejection letter. The character in the poem has just been informed that she has failed her comprehensive exams. The lines of the poem are short and disjointed as though the woman could only comprehend the bad news in small bits. Interspersed between lines from the letter are phrases that offer clues to her state of mind, "regret sorry that you have / failed / your hair should have been / piled up higher."

➤ The scenario of this poem may be foreign to many students. Offer them background information about comprehensive exams for university doctoral programs. It is important that students understand how much work would have gone into a candidate's studies in order to reach this academic level. This will help them make sense of what the woman in the poem is feeling — shock, dismay, bitterness, frustration.

FOR DISCUSSION AND REFLECTION

➤ Ask students to reread the poem, underlining the words that they think actually appeared in the letter. Do these phrases form complete sentences? (No, the woman is hardly able to focus enough to make the words come together in logical order.)

➤ Have students find lines that are broken in surprising places — for example, "the unsuccessfully completed best / wishes for the future." What clues do such breaks give you to the woman's state of mind? (In this case it expresses irony. What she completed was her best. The university's wishes for her future are anything but the "best.")

Writing

QUICK ASSESS

Do students' letters:

✓ maintain an appropriate tone?

✓ include adequate details?

Students are asked to imagine the moment of disappointment when they have just been rejected for something they really wanted. Encourage them to think about tone as they compose the rejection letters they might have received.

READING AND WRITING EXTENSIONS

➤ Have students write the text of what they think the actual letter of rejection in the poem contained. Encourage them to use information from the poem as well as their imagination to fill in what has been omitted.

➤ Divide the class into groups and have each group prepare a reading of "You Understand the Requirements." The lines may be divided among readers, or the group can coach one reader to present for them. After students have heard the various oral presentations of the poem, discuss how each of these is an interpretation of the poem's tone.

Three Comparing Poems

Critical Reading

BACKGROUND

Tone is an aspect of all spoken and written statements — from earnest declarations of love to a subpoena to appear in court, from a Publisher's Clearinghouse million dollar award notice to a neighbor's complaint over loud music. As a literary concept, tone is adapted from the phrase "tone of voice" and reflects a writer's attitude toward an object or a situation as well as toward the reader.

➤ This lesson invites students to compare how W. H. Auden and Lyn Lifshin have achieved the tone they sought in "The Unknown Citizen" and "You Understand the Requirements." Using very different tones, both poems critique the norms of society. Both demonstrate how rules and requirements can stifle creativity, leaving little room for individuals within the system. Both also use an imaginary official document as a basis for a poem.

FOR DISCUSSION AND REFLECTION

➤ What role did the character who says the lines (the persona) play in your reading of the poems? Does the speaker seem intelligent or stupid, friendly or unfriendly, reliable or unreliable, idealistic or pragmatic? (Auden's speaker is 100% bureaucrat. Lifshin's speaker is a doctoral candidate who has just been informed that she may not continue at the university. She is distraught.)

➤ How would you describe Auden and Lifshin's attitude towards you, the reader? (Both assume an intelligent reader who will be able to see between the lines of their poems. They both require careful reading to grasp the situation and message.)

Writing

Students are asked to compare the ways the two writers use scenario, persona, sentence patterns, and diction to convey tone. As a prewriting exercise, divide the class into four groups and assign each group one of these terms to define in their own words. Post the definitions where all can see and use them as they write.

READING AND WRITING EXTENSIONS

➤ Almost all readers enjoy poems with a humorous tone. Reread Ogden Nash's short poem on page 184 and discuss how he achieves his tone using only twelve words. Read students other poems by Ogden Nash.

➤ In "Doggerel by a Senior Citizen," W. H. Auden puts his own critique of the 1960s into the mouth of an old geezer: "Our earth in 1969 / Is not the planet I call mine, / The world, I mean, that gives me strength / To hold off chaos at arm's length." Ask students to write an explanation of Auden's tone in this stanza:

> Dare any call Permissiveness
> An educational success?
> Saner those class-rooms which I sat in,
> Compelled to study Greek and Latin.

Four Using Metaphors

Critical Reading

FOCUS

From *Einstein's Dreams*:

"There is a place where time stands still. Raindrops hang motionless in air. Pendulums of clocks float mid-swing. Dogs raise their muzzles in silent howls."

Writers often explain complicated ideas through metaphors.

BACKGROUND

Alan Lightman's novel *Einstein's Dreams* presents the reader with a series of speculative worlds, all purportedly dreamed by the young patent clerk Albert Einstein, all about the nature of time. Michiko Kakutani called the book "whimsical and meditative, playful and provocative. It pulls the reader into a dream world like a powerful magnet." Part of the reason we are drawn into this world is a result of Lightman's seductive tone. We want to understand time, and Lightman lures us into new ways of thinking about it.

FOR DISCUSSION AND REFLECTION

➤ Ask students to think about occasions when time seemed to speed up (a day at Disneyland, a rock concert, an hour with a great friend) and occasions when time seemed to slow down (a baseball game when their team is way behind, a boring history class, waiting for a bus in bad weather). Make two lists on the board and then ask students what the occasions in each column seem to have in common. Has time really sped up or slowed down? (The answer here is "of course not," but push students to think about the nature of perception.)

➤ Have students close their eyes and read the first paragraph of this excerpt aloud to them. Invite them to picture what they hear in their minds' eye. (Like Magritte's surrealist paintings, the fact that these are "impossible" images only serves to make them the more intriguing.)

➤ According to Lightman, what kind of people would want to be frozen in time? (Possible responses include parents who don't want to see their children grow up, grow old, or ever get hurt and lovers in the throes of a grand passion.)

Writing

QUICK ASSESS

Do students' writings:

✔ identify two positive and two negative images?

✔ explain why and how certain lines struck them?

As students put together a collection of passages that convey the concept of timelessness vividly for them, have them share their reasons for choosing these particular lines. Often it is easier to explain reasons in conversation than to list them on paper.

READING AND WRITING EXTENSIONS

➤ Have students research Albert Einstein and report to the class what they have learned about what he was like as a young man and his studies of the nature of time.

➤ Alan Lightman is a physicist and writing instructor at MIT in Cambridge, Massachusetts. Have students write letters to the author expressing their responses to this story as well as any other ideas or images they can come up with for depicting the concept of timelessness.

Five The Paralog

Critical Reading

FOCUS

A paralog refers to a piece of writing in which a reader responds directly to the author, either line by line or section by section. The result is a piece of writing in two voices: the author's and the reader's.

BACKGROUND

Reader response theory is an attempt to account for the role played by the reader when interpreting literature. It recognizes that readings of any given work differ greatly from reader to reader and that readings are affected by the reader's gender, age, cultural background, personal life experiences, and beliefs, as well as his or her past experiences with literature.

➤ Students with very little experience with literary texts often feel that authors are purposely evasive about saying what they mean and that their teachers have somewhere hidden in their desks a book with all the answers. The paralog exercise described in this lesson may help disabuse students of this view by validating their personal responses to a piece of rich and difficult literature.

FOR DISCUSSION AND REFLECTION

➤ Ask students to share aloud the lines they have underlined in the excerpt from *Einstein's Dreams*. What qualities do these words and phrases have in common? (Often students will choose lines that puzzle them or perplex them with a new idea. They choose phrases that are in some way luminous.)

➤ Have a student choose a classmate's line and tell what it caused him or her to see or feel. Ask the person who chose the line originally what the line made him or her see or feel. Discuss how various responses to lines can be valid.

Writing

QUICK ASSESS

Do students' paralogs:

✓ contain lines from the excerpt that inspired rich responses?

✓ make their lines sound as though they were answering the author's phrases?

✓ maintain a consistent tone?

Students are asked to create a paralog using lines from Lightman's writing and their own responses to these lines. In order to offer students a model of a paralog, choose another chapter from *Einstein's Dreams* or any other rich prose passage and create a paralog on the board with students watching. Using the passage they are going to work with may cause students to feel that your paralog is the "correct" one and will be likely to stifle their own responses.

READING AND WRITING EXTENSIONS

➤ Ask students to turn back through the pages of this book to find a poem or story that they liked very much and would be interested in using for another paralog. Follow the same directions as those provided for *Einstein's Dreams*.

➤ As a twist, have students pull another textbook out of their backpacks and have them create a paralog using lines from their Spanish or biology or social studies books. Collect these paralogs in a class booklet or post them on the bulletin board.

Unit Overview

In this unit, students will explore the world of African American anthropologist and author Zora Neale Hurston. As they read and respond to excerpts from a memoir, a collection of folklore, and a novel, students will examine methods of character development, look at variations in point of view, and consider the emphasis Hurston places on her cultural heritage.

Literature Focus

	Lesson	Literature
1.	The Autobiographical Narrator	from "How It Feels To Be Colored Me" (Nonfiction)
2.	In Search of Her People's History	"How God Made Butterflies" from *Mules and Men* (Nonfiction)
3.	Creating Characters	from *Their Eyes Were Watching God* (Novel)
4.	Multiple Points of View	from *Their Eyes Were Watching God* (Novel)
5.	The Writer's Themes	

Reading Focus

1. The events, descriptions, opinions, and tone of autobiographical writing reveal the author to the reader.
2. Writers often draw from the storytelling traditions of their own culture for subjects and techniques to use in their own writing.
3. Writers often express their opinions about the qualities of character they admire through the portrayals they present in fiction.
4. Writers use multiple points of view to present a fuller and more complex story.
5. The themes of a writer's work become the basis for readers' explorations of the literary work and their own lives.

Writing Focus

1. Write a paragraph describing what you learned about Hurston from reading an excerpt from her memoir.
2. Use a model to create an explanation story that reflects your cultural heritage.
3. Fill in a characterization chart, and then use it to write a paragraph about how the author depicts her female characters and what qualities she admires in women.
4. Rewrite a paragraph from the excerpt by using a first-person narrator.
5. Write an essay about the central meaning in Hurston's writings, including your personal response to her themes.

One The Autobiographical Narrator

C r i t i c a l   R e a d i n g

FOCUS

When authors write about their past, they give meaning to their present.

BACKGROUND

Zora Neale Hurston (1903–1960) was an African American folklorist and writer who celebrated the culture of the rural South. Born in Eatonville, Florida, she joined a traveling theatrical company at sixteen and ended up in New York City during the Harlem Renaissance. She studied anthropology with Franz Boas at Columbia University and traveled in the South collecting the stories that people told. In Haiti, she studied voodoo. Ultimately Hurston rejected the scholarly approach to ethnic study in favor of a more personal one. In 1931 she wrote a play, *Mule Bone*, with Langston Hughes; in 1934 she published her first novel, *Jonah's Gourd Vine;* and in 1937 she published her widely acclaimed and (at the time) highly controversial novel, *Their Eyes Were Watching God.*

FOR DISCUSSION AND REFLECTION

➤ How does the tone of the first paragraph of "How It Feels To Be Colored Me" offer you a clue to what Hurston's attitude will be in this piece? (Though many African Americans have Native American blood, she pokes gentle fun at those who feel the need for an Indian chief in their ancestry to validate their own stature and worth. Hurston feels worthy just as she is.)

➤ Based upon your sense of the voice in this essay, how old do you think Hurston was when she wrote it? (She was twenty-five years old. Students may have observed that she had enough distance from her childhood to be able to write about it with objectivity. Hurston's voice in this essay is one of indomitable energy and optimism. This outlook often characterizes young, talented, ambitious writers.)

➤ What does Hurston mean when she says in the sixth paragraph that she is "not tragically colored"? (She refuses to endorse the myth of black inferiority, but neither does she see herself as a victim of this myth.)

W r i t i n g

QUICK ASSESS

Do students' paragraphs:

✓ identify important autobiographical information in the essay?

✓ discuss qualities and experiences that a writer might need?

Students are asked to write a paragraph explaining the things they learned about Hurston from her essay and to explore how the qualities she possessed and the experiences she had could be valuable to a writer. Have students brainstorm the qualities and experiences that they think writers need. When contradictory characteristics are offered, include both — for example, introspective/outgoing or hardworking/a dreamer.

READING AND WRITING EXTENSIONS

➤ The 1979 anthology of Zora Neale Hurston's work was titled *I Love Myself When I Am Laughing…and Then Again When I Am Looking Mean and Impressive.* After explaining to students what an anthology typically contains, ask them to speculate on what a title like this suggests about the author whose work it contains.

➤ Reread the last paragraph of "How It Feels To Be Colored Me" and then invite students to imagine themselves as a "bag of miscellany" and describe the contents of this bag.

Two In Search of Her People's History

Critical Reading

FOCUS
Zora Neale Hurston on folklore:

"Folklore is the art that people create before they know there is such a thing as art."

BACKGROUND
In her autobiography, *Dust Tracks on a Road,* Zora Neale Hurston describes her work with Franz Boas: "I was extremely proud that Papa Franz felt like sending me on that folklore search. As is well known, Dr. Franz Boas, of the Department of Anthropology of Columbia University, is the greatest anthropologist alive, for two reasons. The first is his insatiable hunger for knowledge and then more knowledge; and the second is his genius for pure objectivity. He has no pet wishes to prove. His instructions are to go out and find what is there."

➤ "How God Made Butterflies" is one of the stories Hurston collected in her research.

FOR DISCUSSION AND REFLECTION
➤ For some students, the dialect that Hurston uses to retell the story of "How God Made Butterflies" may prove a challenge. Put a list of words with unconventional spellings (*de* for *the, wuz* for *was, Lawd* for *Lord, tole* for *told, dere* for *there*) on the board and have students figure out their meanings and look for patterns (*d* for *th,* for example).

➤ Why do you think storytellers create such tales? (Possible responses include to explain the workings of the natural world, to entertain themselves and their children, as an outlet for their own creative imaginations.)

➤ What do you think Hurston learned from collecting stories such as "How God Made Butterflies" that she would be able to use later in her own writing? (a sensitivity to the nuances of language, an ear for the poetry in speech, the power of imaginative answers to intellectual questions, and the appreciation for the art of storytelling)

Writing

QUICK ASSESS
Do students' stories:

✓ explain a natural phenomenon?

✓ combine factual and imaginative truth?

✓ reflect values or mores of one type or another?

Students are asked to construct a story of their own that explains a natural phenomenon. Before they begin to write, have students brainstorm a list of seemingly inexplicable aspects of the natural world. Given that we live in a scientific age in which biologists and physicists have found explanations for many of the things that once amazed us, urge students to imagine the world through the eyes of a child.

READING AND WRITING EXTENSIONS
➤ Have students research folklore from other cultures in which natural phenomena are explained through stories. Greek and West African mythology are rich in such tales.

➤ Invite students to become researchers of stories from their own culture. Have students ask a parent or grandparent or friend to retell an old story. Have them ask the storyteller for permission to make a tape recording of the story and then share it with the class. Like good ethnographers, they should identify the date and place and teller of the story with care.

Three Creating Characters

Critical Reading

FOCUS

From *The Signifying Monkey* by Henry Louis Gates, Jr:

"Their Eyes Were Watching God depicts the search for identity and self-understanding of an Afro-American woman."*

BACKGROUND

Henry Louis Gates, Jr., has written that "the narrative voice Hurston created, and her legacy to Afro-American fiction, is a lyrical and disembodied yet individual voice, from which emerges a singular longing and utterance, a transcendent, ultimately racial self, extending far beyond the merely individual. Hurston realized a resonant and authentic narrative voice that echoes and aspires to the stature of the impersonality, selfless tradition, at once collective and compelling, true somehow to the unwritten text of a common blackness. For Hurston, the search for a telling form of language, indeed the search for a black literary language itself, defines the search for self." *(The Signifying Monkey)*

➤ In this excerpt from the opening of *Their Eyes Were Watching God,* Hurston gives readers a vivid picture of Janie Walker, Pheoby (her best friend), and the people on the porch. Almost like a Greek chorus, the porch watchers provide a running commentary on Janie's return.

FOR DISCUSSION AND REFLECTION

➤ The first two paragraphs of this excerpt compare the life of men with the life of women. Explain Hurston's metaphor. (Men are dreamers, content to wait and see if their wishes "come in with the tide" or "remain forever on the horizon." Women are practical, making pragmatic decisions about how they choose their dreams; "they act.")

➤ How does Pheoby demonstrate her friendship with Janie? (She defends her to the people on the porch, brings her food, listens to her story.)

Writing

QUICK ASSESS

Do students' paragraphs:

✔ identify the techniques Hurston has used to make these characters come to life?

✔ discuss what qualities in women Hurston admires?

✔ draw on specific passages as support?

Based upon their reading of this excerpt, students are asked to describe how Hurston characterizes the women in her story and discuss the qualities Hurston admires in women. List some of the techniques that storytellers use to reveal character on the board: descriptions of appearance, references to their actions, quotes from the character, quotes of what others say about the character.

READING AND WRITING EXTENSIONS

➤ Ask students to imagine their best friend has just returned after several years away from home. Write an interior monologue describing what would be going on inside their head on the way to see this person. What would they be wondering about? What questions would they plan to ask?

➤ Can students think of a time when they felt people were watching them critically and talking about them? This might be a time when they were up at bat, in front of the class making a presentation, at a dance or music recital. Have them describe how they felt.

Four Multiple Points of View

Critical Reading

FOCUS

From *The Signifying Monkey* by Henry Louis Gates, Jr.:

"Janie uses the metaphor of the tree to define her own desires but also to mark the distance of those with whom she lives from these desires."

BACKGROUND

The third-person point of view is the most widely used, probably because it is the most adaptable. It assumes a neutral and objective stance. The narrator is presumed to be the author, standing outside the events of the story. *Omniscient* comes from the Greek word for "all knowing." Thus an omniscient narrator has access to every thought and emotion of the characters.

➤ In this famous pear tree passage, Janie's emerging sexual awareness is described through lush and compelling tree imagery. To "be a pear tree — any tree in bloom" is an expression of Janie's desire to experience life fully.

FOR DISCUSSION AND REFLECTION

➤ Why do you think Janie would choose to begin the story to Pheoby with a description of a spring afternoon "under a blossoming pear tree"? (This moment represents for Janie an awakening. She feels touched by life and knows that although she is not yet a woman, she is no longer a child.)

➤ How has "shiftless Johnny Taylor" suddenly become "beglamored" in Janie's eyes? (She was "looking, waiting, breathing short with impatience" when suddenly he appeared in the road. Anything other than the sameness of life with Nanny appears desirable to her now.)

Writing

QUICK ASSESS

Do students' revisions:

✓ consistently use first-person point of view?

✓ convey the content and tone of the original?

Students are asked to rewrite a paragraph from the excerpt as though Janie were speaking directly to Pheoby the way she did in the earlier excerpt. Before students begin to write, discuss how the shift from the third person (Janie as "she") to the first person (Janie to herself as "I") is likely to affect the reader.

READING AND WRITING EXTENSIONS

➤ In her autobiography, *Dust Tracks on a Road*, Hurston writes: "I wrote *Their Eyes Were Watching God* in Haiti. It was dammed up in me, and I wrote it under internal pressure in seven weeks. I wish that I could write it again. In fact, I regret all of my books. It is one of the tragedies of life that one cannot have all the wisdom one is ever to possess in the beginning. Perhaps, it is just as well to be rash and foolish for a while. If writers were too wise, perhaps no books would be written at all." Read this quote to students and discuss whether they agree or disagree with Hurston about authors being "rash and foolish" when they write.

➤ Have students write about a time when something that they saw in nature — a dead animal, a beautiful sunset, a thundering sky, a street covered with newly fallen snow — caused them to reflect upon their own life.

Five The Writer's Themes

Critical Reading

FOCUS

Zora Neale Hurston on writing:

"When I began to make up stories I cannot say. Just from one fancy to another, adding more and more detail until they seemed real."

BACKGROUND

Zora Neale Hurston died in poverty in a Florida welfare home in 1960. At the time she died, all her books were out of print. It was not until the late seventies with the diligence of Alice Walker, Robert Hemenway, and others that Hurston's work resurfaced. Since that time many critical studies have been written, often focusing on Janie as a questing female character in relation to Hurston's own difficult life as an African American woman artist.

➤ This lesson invites students to review the selections and to consider what these passages suggest about Hurston as a writer. For Hurston, "The force from somewhere in space which commands you to write in the first place gives you no choice. You take up the pen when you are told, and write what is commanded. There is no agony like bearing an untold story inside you."

FOR DISCUSSION AND REFLECTION

➤ Based upon your reading of "How It Feels To Be Colored Me," is Zora Neale Hurston the kind of person you would be interested in getting to know? Why or why not? (Responses will vary.)

➤ What does "How God Made Butterflies" suggest about Hurston as a writer? (This is someone with tremendous respect for the language and culture of her people. She celebrates words and sees them as a source of power. Hurston also has a lively sense of humor.)

➤ If you were Pheoby, do you think you would want to hear Janie's story? (Point out to students who say 'yes' that they might want to read *Their Eyes Were Watching God*.)

Writing

QUICK ASSESS

Do students' essays:

✓ focus on Hurston's central theme?

✓ use specifics from a range of selections as support?

✓ suggest what effects Hurston's writing had upon them as readers?

Students are asked to write an essay discussing Hurston's themes as well as the meanings that they take away from their reading of her stories. It may help to create two clusters: one of what students learned, the other of what they still want to know.

READING AND WRITING EXTENSIONS

➤ Invite students to imagine their former fifth-grade teacher saw them carrying a book by Zora Neale Hurston home from the library and asked what made them choose this author to read. What would they tell her?

➤ *In Dust Tracks on a Road,* Hurston describes her initial failure as an ethnographer: "My first six months were disappointing. I found out later that it was not because I had not talents for research, but because I did not have the right approach. The glamour of Barnard College was still upon me. I knew where the material was all right. But, I went about asking, in carefully accented Barnardese, 'Pardon me, but do you know any folk-tales or folk-songs?' The men and women who had whole treasuries of material just seeping through their pores looked at me and shook their heads." Discuss what students are able to infer about Hurston from the folk tale "How God Made Butterflies" and from what they have learned about her work as a collector of folk tales.

I n d e x

Teacher's Guide page numbers are in parentheses following pupil's edition page numbers.

Lesson Title Index

Literature Index